Voices of
Practitioner Scholars
in Management

Voices of Practitioner Scholars in Management

The History and Impact of the
Doctor of Management Programs at
Case Western Reserve University

Edited by Philip A. Cola, Kalle J. Lyytinen and S.A. Nartker

ORANGE *frazer* PRESS
Wilmington, Ohio

ISBN 978-1949248-210
Copyright©2020 Case Western Reserve University
All Rights Reserved

Published for
Weatherhead School of Management
Case Western Reserve University
by: Orange Frazer Press

For price and shipping information, call: Sue Nartker at Case Western Reserve University at 216.368.1943

Book and cover design by: Karen Davison and Case Western Reserve University

Library of Congress Control Number: 2020901000

First Printing

Contents

Introductory Notes

Philip A. Cola, PhD
Kalle Lyytinen, PhD

This book embodies the plurality of exciting thinking and unique lived experiences as expressed in the voices of management practitioner scholars who completed the Doctor of Management (DM) programs at Case Western Reserve University (CWRU) during the last quarter of a century. These voices were collected and organized into a chorus of stories during the planning of the 25th Anniversary of the DM programs at CWRU. The programs have been a global market leader in the engagement in and production of "research that matters" in management since their inception. The programs were the first to introduce the residency-based interdisciplinary doctoral curriculum, which drew intellectual inspiration from a wide range of social science theories and research methods while seeking to integrate high levels of rigor with real world relevance in management settings.

This book manifests the concerted effort of the management practitioner-scholar community within CWRU to increase awareness of what this community has achieved during its quarter century existence. The book originates from the proposal by the former Dean of the Weatherhead School of Management, Dr. Mohan Reddy, who asked us to collect and report as part of the 25-year celebration the research conducted in the program and how it has helped to address specific management challenges. This initial request grew into a book that conveys a rich story of what participating in the Doctor of Management programs means as a lived experience and what types of intellectual challenges are faced by the students and alumni after graduation. It also reports and demonstrates the wide range of outcomes and deliverables that have emerged from this effort over time that reach well beyond the theses and conference articles produced during the study period. It also conveys a story of what have been the real world implications of the programs for many participating managers and organizations. It is our hope to provide the book to appropriate audiences as identified by our alumni, faculty and the external communities who can benefit from the sharing of the experiences and the research that has come out of the DM programs.

The voices that follow represent voluntary contributions of DM alumni. To invite such contributions we sent out a solicitation call to all DM programs graduates (nearly 300 total) to ask for their help in promoting the work and the impact of the DM programs through their personal stories related to their program study and especially their research during and after graduation. They were specifically asked to send us a two-page summary of their research and experiences focused on: 1) the practitioner audience that has most likely benefited from their research and experience; and 2) how their work has furthered management practice to particular management audiences. The major goal of the solicitation was to learn about and translate the information emanating from DM-based practitioner scholarship for other stakeholders of the program who can benefit from and use the information for better management practices. These include other managers, potential students, research organizations, and funding agencies. We received an overwhelming response of more than 60 candidate authors (the response rate of more than 20%) who initially "pitched" their narrative for the inclusion in the book.

The solicitations were reviewed by a committee consisting of DM alumni, faculty and staff (9 members in total). The committee reviewed the initial proposals and gave detailed feedback to candidate authors. Based on the authors' response, the committee decided to cull the final voices to be included in the book to approximately 25–30 narratives. Our long-term goal is, however, to publish additional volumes of DM narratives.

We informed the selected candidates to write a longer (5–6 page double-spaced or approximately 3,000 words) full narrative of their research experience that would comply with a pre-defined style guidelines that the editorial committee had created and approved. The guidelines sought to ensure the uniformity of the voices in terms of the narrative length, scope and style. The more specific invitation resulted in 36 final narrative documents submitted for consideration. The complete narratives were submitted to the committee for additional feedback, which was also shared with the authors. A 23-step process was initiated and moved the voices from idea solicitation to the 27 final narratives that occupy the pages this book. We experienced some attrition when the initial 36 submissions were reduced to 27 final voices. The attrition emerged mostly from author time constraints related to publishing deadlines for printing the book in time for the 25ᵗʰ anniversary celebration.

We recruited professional copy editors to work with each submitted narrative to refine the style and add punch to the voices. Simultaneously, we identified a designer, through a DM programs alumna who is a design expert, to help us create the uniform design, style and flow of the book that would express the goals and ideas about the book as conveyed by the editors. The editors also selected the publisher and processed the agreements and contracts. An enjoyable aspect of putting this book together was the ability to design and innovate along the way in the spirit of the ethos found in the DM programs. After reading many stories and thinking about how to organize the materials for the book, we came up with the idea to divide the book into the six personas that serve as separate sections to categorize the book into multiple themes of what it means to be a DM student and alumna.

Similarly, we got the idea for the writing stories of the personal experiences by the DM academic directors who set the stage for the programs. Not surprisingly and in the spirit of grounded method, these personas emerged organically from reading the writings of the authors while making sense and giving sense to them. We thought what types of behaviors and aspirations potentially lie behind these stories; what are the psychological and individual "gestalts" of the alumni voices? After some dialogue and re-interpretation, we identified the personas of Learners, Explorers, Educators, Connectors, Innovators and Dreamers. As you read the personal journeys and voices of the DM alumni, we hope you can clearly see how each of these personas act and think and how they manifest one repertoire of behaviors enabled by the DM programs. These personas might also help you formulate your future vision of what you want your personal journey to be in your life. Many of authors actually fit into multiple personas (as many people are filled with multiple personas), but as editors, we had to choose which one was the dominating persona in each narrative. We hope you agree with our judgment. Overall, this reading and sense-giving was a truly fun part of this editorial process and it marked a period of important learning and discovery for us about what it means to be a DM student and alumnus.

We hope that listening to the DM voices will be advantageous across multiple dimensions including: 1) provisioning of a dissemination outlet that highlights the great stories and the work of DM alumni; 2) demonstrating the value creation that has accrued by the deeds and efforts of the DM alumni to the practitioner communities. This may lead to recruiting new candidates for the DM Programs who want to follow the footsteps of some of the alumni; 3) building awareness about the value of "engaged management", "practitioner scholarship", and "research that matters". These terms are frequently used in academic settings, but it is not always easy to convey in concrete terms what they mean in the practitioner community. We hope this book fulfils some of this gap. This book has been an interesting and strange learning journey to us personally.

Dr. Kalle Lyytinen, one of the editors has been the director of the DM Programs for over a decade. He has read most of the outputs and dissertations of the people who have lent their voices to the book. He has also acted as the personal mentor and advisor to many of these alumni including Dr. Phil Cola, a co-editor. It has been an awakening moment and genuine experience to read and hear about the personal experiences of the alumni, what they learned, and how they experienced life during and after the program. We learned to appreciate more the grit and the intellect of the alumni. Dr. Cola is a DM Programs graduate and now serves as the Associate Director and faculty member for the DM Programs. This position surely qualifies him to obtain a unique perspective about the relevance and impact of the DM Programs. Yet, several surprises took place. First, Phil did not know what he was getting into when Kalle asked him to "help" with editing the book, as he had never done this before. Admittedly, this process has been overwhelming at times and more complex than initially was thought. Second, he saw this editor role as an opportunity to highlight stories of what he believes to be a uniquely exceptional doctoral program. He, however, realized during the process that he would have never achieved his own long-standing dream, his ideal future, of being a triple-threat faculty member who teaches, conducts research and provides organizational service to a prestigious university, if it was not for the DM Programs that he found right in his own backyard at CWRU. The opportunities granted to him from his association with the DM Programs have turned out to be truly limitless. Therefore, Phil eagerly wants to share the voices of others as to why this program is, indeed, exceptional.

Finally, we hope this book brings all readers closer to a fascinating and diverse reality and the lived experiences of truly outstanding practitioner scholars who have been our colleagues, friends, students, and companions during the 25-year journey of the DM programs. We ask that you openly listen to the stories that follow in the Voices of Practitioner Scholars in Management and experience the thrill as we did while listening to them!

Acknowledgments

We are grateful for the help of many individuals without whom this book would not have been possible. First, thanks to the earlier DM Programs Directors — Drs. John Aram, Bo Carlsson — for their interest and support. We also wish to thank the visionary founding fathers of the DM Programs — Drs. John Aram, Scott Cowen, Richard Boland, Richard Boyatzis, Bo Carlsson, Mohan Reddy, Paul Salipante, and Jagdip Singh for their ideas and support during the evolution of the DM Programs. These individuals globally changed the course of tertiary doctoral education in management by envisioning the DM Programs, though at the time it was conceived a wild and odd idea. There is not enough time, space, or words to express the gratitude that we owe to each of them.

Sincere appreciation and gratitude to our fellow reviewers and copy editors — Drs. Mariana Amatullo, Bernard Bailey, Kevin Cavanagh, Eileen Doherty-Sil, Beth Fitz Gibbon, and Ann Kowal Smith. We also thank the hard work, understanding and patience, of our wonderful graphics and layout designer, Karen Davison. It was truly a pleasure working with you! We also thank the nearly limitless effort and support we received from Sue Nartker, Marilyn Chorman and Rochelle Muchnicki. We also thank Joshua Gerlick (current DM student) for his last minute assistance with formatting the reference section of the book.

Finally, we thank our amazing alumni, who continue to change management practices every day through their innovative evidence-based practices. We are especially grateful to those who were able to take the time to write the narratives during their busy lives, as they did not know what they were getting into in terms of the expected amount of work. We are personally grateful for their patience in working with the editors while we shaped and moved their stories forward. It was enormously gratifying to get to know on a personal level (even if virtually) many people that have made these programs so exceptional.

Voices of
Practitioner Scholars
in Management

"*Live as if you were to die tomorrow. Learn as if you were to live forever.*"

Mahatma Gandhi

Learner

Developing the skills and
desire for lifelong learning

Michael J. Barnes

The whole entering class of 1996 bonded immediately. From California, throughout Ohio, to Virginia and Missouri and across the Atlantic, we converged on CWRU for our required doctoral residencies for three memorable years. These became the touchstone for learning, and each member of the fellowship held each other with the highest regard and utmost respect — lightened with necessary doses of good humor and sometimes hilarity.

An EDM Odyssey

Dr. John Aram was the most influential teacher of my life. I first met John in early 1995 at London's Heathrow airport. He was in transit from Boston to India, meeting up with Dr. Mohan Reddy to do some consulting with the iron and steel industry there.

I had caught sight of an attractive advertisement in *The Economist* announcing the launch of a unique concept in higher education: The Executive Doctor of Management (EDM) program (now called the Doctor of Management program) for experienced practitioner-scholars, offered for the first time by the Weatherhead School of Management at Case Western Reserve University (CWRU) in Cleveland, Ohio. Although I had lived and worked in the U.S. for nine years previously, I knew little about Cleveland or CWRU. However, the announcement grabbed my attention and I immediately applied. I was then a First Vice President at Union Bank of Switzerland (UBS).

John offered me admission and I was thrilled to accept. Later, upon reflection and discussion with family, I requested a deferral because I thought the commute from Zurich to Cleveland for three years would be too costly and time-consuming on top of tuition (we were still recovering financially from my Stanford MBA).

However, one year later, Dr. Aram inquired again if I wanted to attend the DM. By then I had returned to my hometown of London and earned a comfortable living as a director of Lazard Asset Management. Again,

I jumped at the opportunity, but asked if I might sit in on one of the weekend residencies of the pathfinders entering class of 1995 to which I had been admitted earlier. Moreover, I was not disappointed.

Five Lessons from the 20th Century for 25 Years On
1. When AI was Appreciative Inquiry

Spending a weekend as participant observer with the 1995 cohort of 'DM Trailblazers' was a true revelation. It was so exciting just to hear the crackle and see the sparks of evening discussion between all the contributors — students and faculty alike. I remember very clearly Dr. David Cooperrider sharing his groundbreaking thoughts, ideas, and research about Appreciative Inquiry (AI); the intellectual stimulation provided by Drs. Paul Salipante and Aram; the global insights provided by Dr. Bo Carlsson. This is what "continuous learning and self-improvement" is all about: "Tell me a story about when you were at the peak of your performance and firing on all cylinders." Not: please list your strengths and weaknesses in the boxes below.

2. When Emotional Intelligence (EI) was in its Infancy

I could see and hear Dr. Richard Boyatzis formulating his concepts and constructs to advance the theory and interpretation of Emotional Intelligence and its role in creating resonance and leadership. Walking one mile in the other fellow's shoes (which also has the advantage of being a mile away when he realizes you have got his shoes) is being able to appreciate someone else's point of view, circumstance, culture, ideology, and religion.

The whole entering class of 1996 bonded immediately. From California, throughout Ohio, to Virginia and Missouri and across the Atlantic, we converged on CWRU for our required doctoral residencies for three memorable years. These became the touchstone for learning, and each member of the fellowship held each other with the highest regard and utmost respect — lightened with necessary doses of good humor and sometimes hilarity.

My 20-year journey since then has not quite taken me full circle geographically speaking, but I was reminded recently how learning is really about "educere" in Latin: to draw or "lead out" from oneself what one already knows. I had forgotten one of the key theories of "Leadership" that I had developed in the DM program at CWRU, that L= f(T,r) or Leadership is a joint function of TrustBuilding and Risk Taking. Along the way I also learned that leading is about listening and "Shaping Expectations" per my late boss, Dr. Manesh Shrikant, founding father of S P Jain Institute of Management & Research, Mumbai. Most recently, I learned from my colleague at SRM University, Dr. Jamshed Barucha, former president of Cooper Union and academic leader at Dartmouth College and Tufts University that "the dirty little secret about learning" (available on YouTube) is that

The DM Program had given me the courage and confidence to break out of my old mold, to explore new concepts, constructs, and contexts.

we forget. First, you actively learn by doing (Action Learning was my first university appointment at CWRU in 2000) after that you quickly forget; then you gradually re-learn by remembering. Learning is remembrance.

3. Group Dynamics in Learning and Listening

A very good friend and former DM program cohort member in my class would frequently intervene by saying: "So, Michael, what is your point?" Repeated humiliation in this manner led me to realize that learning is about careful, appreciative listening – and not subconsciously trying to dominate the discussion through "additional air-time". I also learned that in collaborating "two heads are better than one". I learned so much, the ability to intellectually probe, how to consistently be prepared, and how to use my experience in a practical way from my dear DM program cohort members. We each have our own particular skills, insights, and abilities that can complement one another. Another great supporter from the cohort who helped me enormously was a very soft spoken gentleman who had extensive experience in aeronautics. Without his patient guidance and encouragement in helping me navigate statistical software, I may never have arrived at my destination. Although, I always had an instinctive "feel" for quantitative analyses, it was never my forte when it came to getting the precise answer. Precision in fact has become one of my required "7Ps" for becoming a true professional, alongside being Positive, Prepared, Persistent, Patient, Polite, and Punctual.

4. Continuous Education and Self Improvement

When you are in the higher education space as I have been for the past twenty years or so "continuous improvement" becomes a bit of a mantra for accreditation purposes (like "cutting-edge research"). But if signing up for the DM program is the first big step towards subscribing to the need for continuous education and self improvement then completing the degree is the first step toward a lifetime of learning based on reflexive practice and a dedication to concentrated hard work and academic commitment. I learn something new every day: sometimes big, sometimes small. But the DM program opened my eyes to the "Great Other" to which I was unaware during my preceding 25 years of being a so-called 20th century international banker — when the profession was still marginally respectable.

5. Learning from Life before Google, Excel, and SPSS

After my wonderful four years as the inaugural John F. Fiedler/ BorgWarner Endowed Chair of Global Business Studies at Kent State University, I have had the great privilege and satisfaction since 2007 to be the creator and founding dean of MBA, BBA, and B. Com (Hons.) programs in Dubai, India (twice) and Vietnam, as well as Principal of The British College in my all-time favorite, Nepal. In addition, I often greet new students offering some variation of the following:

> In today's world you can Google almost all factual knowledge, but you cannot Google good judgment, wisdom, integrity, creativity and innovation, leadership and communications skills, team-working ability, or the values that underpin ethical management and decision-making.

> Tolerance for ambiguity, embracing diversity of thought and culture are not learned on the Internet. They are learned through hard work, extensive practice, methodical inquiry, personal evidence gathering and observation, reflection, and the application of sound analytical principles that rest on strong, tested, conceptual foundations. Forget about Massive Open Online Courses (MOOCs) for a moment. Much of the discovery and "knowledge creation" process takes place in the classroom as a laboratory through concentrated face-to-face interaction between

faculty members who are well-grounded in academic research, and students who are often experienced in practices that are even ahead of subsequent academic research and analysis.

Research and useful production are about "Breaking the Template" which sometimes becomes an ironclad intellectual straitjacket. "Cut-and-paste" bruises the imagination and merely skims the surface of knowledge, not to mention self-knowledge. All too often I have seen this with PhD presentations about not very interesting subjects that are merely pre-programmed gymnastic lessons in statistical exercise and contortions worthy of gold medalist Nadia Comaneci, but which nevertheless leave one with the burning question (forget about statistical significance, data sample and error for a moment). *"What is the real significance of the question and what is the important meaning of the answer?"*

My early fears or concerns about the mandatory residencies were totally unwarranted. In fact, those mutual learning opportunities for team working and team-building formed the backbone of the DM experience.

I shall always remember bumping into Drs. Aram and Salipante one snowy day in late November 1997. Dr. Aram asked me if I had decided on a research subject or framed my research question yet. I said, "No, not yet, but I want it to be big, and I want it to be important."

After my return to England some days later, I knew in a flash what I was searching for. The front page in the serious newspaper *The Independent* in early December 1997 featured a lurid pink sky as background to Mount Fuji, with the headline reporting the signing of the Kyoto Protocol on Climate Change. Ten years before Al Gore got his Nobel Prize for his documentary on "An Inconvenient Truth", I decided to write my Applied Research Project on climate change which I entitled "Environomics" for short. This was quite a departure from my 25 years of banking and investments, but the DM Program had given me the courage and confidence to break out of my old mold, to explore new concepts, constructs, and contexts. Some people, I am sure, thought that maybe I had lost my marbles at the time; but my research review panel supported me to the hilt and a new life with new opportunities, vistas, challenges, and global experiences opened up for me. Bingo!

The writing and submission of my final applied research paper in 1998–1999 was an interesting (and sometimes amusing) story in itself. After voraciously reading and buying tons of actual hard-copy books during 1997–1998, I had amassed a large amount of data, evidence, ideas, and precedents that I had no clue what to do with. My father, in July 1998, rewarded and incentivized me for the very last time on my 50th birthday by funding my status as Harvard University's shortest-serving alumnus through attending the very first executive program on Climate Change and Development (CCD) a part of the International Environment Program under Jeffrey Sachs's Harvard Institute for International Development at the John F. Kennedy School of Government.

How to organize the material, and finally write my Applied Research Project (ARP) was the pressing question of the moment. Dr. Salipante had been urging us to experiment with new and different writing styles. Being English, I thought that Shakespeare was different, if not new. So, the first draft of my ARP on "Climate Change in the Last Decade of the 20th Century" was written as a Shakespearean tragedy with the main actors being the EU, USA, Costa Rica, India, Australia, China, Japan, etc. Dr. Aram thought it was an interesting and original approach but counseled me to be a bit more conventional in my second draft.

One night after a long and exhausting reading session, I was sprawled on the couch, subconsciously watching the long and very boring game of snooker being televised on BBC at 2:30 a.m. In a moment of burgundy-assisted serendipity, I realized this was my new metaphor! Dr. Aram had asked us at our very first residency for our own starting-out ideas on a metaphor for the DM Program. I do not know if it was mine, or someone else's suggestion, but I remember the image of riding down helter-skelter the rapids of the Colorado River on one of those giant grey rubber dinghies. Therefore, it was.

To return to my lazy couch and snooker TV, I watched like never before the interaction of the cue ball with the eight colored balls set beforehand in a wooden triangle: yellow, green, brown, blue, pink, black, red, and white. I had always thought the collisions and effects were random and chaotic. Then I thought maybe that is not quite the case. Maybe they are planned and controlled to some extent by the Champion Snooker King?

Believe it or not, I then developed my idea of the Environomic Compass and the less than random interactions between eight domains: the Scientific Academy, International Law, International Politics, National Politics, Domestic Law, Domestic Economic Policy, Multinational Companies, and Environmental Interest Groups (or NGOs). I went back to my beloved Dr. Elinor Ostrom and her inspiring book, *Governing the Commons — The Evolution of Institutions' Collective Action* (1995). Later, she actually autographed my copy when guest lecturing in the Program shortly before winning the Nobel Prize for Economics and her tragic passing away shortly thereafter. I developed what I called the "Foundations of Environomics" somewhat pretentiously after Samuelson's *Foundations of Economics*, based on the many readings on and off the required curriculum devised by Dr. Aram.

This was one of his greatest deep background contributions (with the constant inspiration and suggestions of Paul Salipante) to the entire Weatherhead doctoral program for practitioner scholars: to sow the seeds of curiosity and inquiry. From the required first readings by Graham Allison (1971) on *Essence of Decision*, explaining the Cuban Missile Crisis, to Mancur Olson on *Collective Action* (1995) and Dennis Chong (1991), Edwin Hutchins on *Cognition in the Wild* (1996), Kenichi Ohmae on the *End of the Nation State* (1995), Tom Athanasiou on *Slow Reckoning* (1998), R.H. Coase on *The Problem of Social Cost* (1960), Pierre Bordieu on an *Outline Theory of Practice* (1977), and Fritjof Capra's *The Web of Life* (1996), I was motivated to read the select works of Wittgenstein and write an original paper on 'The Meaning of Red" for Dr. Boland, to write a paper criticizing the ethics of Data Mining and Factor Analysis for Dr. Jagdip Singh; learning about Claude Levi-Strauss and his social anthropological research and theories about "Structuralism"; Francis Fukuyama's *End of History* and Samuel Huntingdon's pre-9/11 *Clash of Civilizations*. Such a rich smorgasbord of opportunity!

The centerpiece of my ARP was probably the eight-step model of the interplay of paradigms (domains) and "Global Regime Formation" following Drs. Ostrom and Nazli Choucri:

Step 1. Problem (Opportunity) Recognition

Step 2. Agenda Setting

Step 3. Institution Building

Step 4. Goal Setting

Step 5. Implementation

Step 6. Regulation

Step 7. Compliance monitoring

Step 8. Enforcement/Conflict Resolution

To quote my ARP:

> These steps are not peculiar to public goods, global commons, or non-market problems. They are equally pertinent, for example, to the setting up of a local stock exchange or a bilateral trade agreement, or a military security pact. The transition from one step to another may be slow or fast. The system's evolution is often surrounded by uncertainty. This may be good or bad. There are non-linearities, interruptions, setbacks, and most of all, recurrent feedback loops which constantly refine, redefine or redirect "The Problem" and associated solutions. Unintended or unexpected consequences and flexible boundaries lead to alternation between tightly-coupled issues or loose coupling (e.g. between climate change and economic development). The organizational reaction to environmental jolts (Meyer 1982) may be strongly influenced by ideologies and market strategies in effective adaptation, whereas the roles that organic structures and slack resources play in adjusting to environmental change may be only weak constraints.

Finally, the big day was upon us and I was presenting my ARP entitled: "Environomics: Global Climate Change Regime Formation and the Interplay of Paradigms in the Last Decade of the 20th Century". I nervously faced the prospect of my Viva Voce with the panel of project advisors chaired by Dr. Reddy, accompanied by Dr. Aram and Professor Wendy Wagner of CWRU School of Law. I had developed my thinking slightly from the static interplay of the "Environomic Compass" via snooker to the more dynamic and complex interplay of paradigms visually represented by the ever-changing colored pattern of a kaleidoscope.

To name but a few, in addition to all my fellow DM program classmates and the Weatherhead DM Faculty of Drs. Aram, Salipante, Reddy, Boyatzis, Boland, Singh, Carlsson, and many others, it was a great privilege and high honor. The faculty and staff at Weatherhead were and are just fabulous, and I shall always be in their debt for helping shape my own life and development over the past 20 years since graduating as part of the DM cohort of 1999.

Keywords
Appreciative Inquiry, Emotional Intelligence, Group Dynamics, Self-Improvement

About the Author: Michael J. Barnes, DM
Dr. Barnes is Professor and Dean of Management at SRM University, AP Amaravati in Andhra Pradesh, India and spent the last 20 years in higher education. Commencing as Assistant Dean of the Weatherhead School at Case Western Reserve University, later as inaugural John F. Fiedler/ BorgWarner Endowed Chair of Global Business at Kent State University, Ohio, his assignments as founding dean of management or principal have taken him to Dubai, Singapore, Vietnam, Nepal, and India.

Leonard Lane

I concluded that leaders in the Imagination Age (sometimes referred to as Industry 4.0 or the digital economy) need to up-scale their capabilities and resiliency as they take on more complex assignments and encounter more complex situations and problems in our increasingly hyper-connected world.

Accelerating Learning in a Whitewater World

One of the important takeaways from the Doctor of Management (DM) program at Case Western Reserve University (CWRU) was not recognized until a few years after I graduated. The takeaway? The capability to read and understand context and build that thinking into my global strategy work. This was beyond conducting an evidence driven Political, Economic, Social, and Technological (PEST) analysis and applying those learnings to industry, company, and competitor analysis. Seeing that we were at a point in time that the world was becoming more complex, volatile, uncertain, ambiguous, and based on the understanding of the need for context as part of learning and doing, I concluded we were at the beginning of another new era as my colleague, John Seely Brown, refers to as the Imagination Age — an age that calls for new ways to see, to imagine, to think, to act, and to learn. The analogy that came to mind for volatile and uncertain was white water kayaking. We are living in a "White Water World" as described by Brown and Pendelton-Jullian (2018) in "Design Unbound: Designing for Emergence in a White Water World".

This world is rapidly moving in often surprising and unforeseen ways. It is radically contingent yet hard to anticipate. It is a world in which we must learn, like a white-water kayaker, to skillfully read the currents and disturbances of the context around you — interpreting the surface flows, ripples, and rapids for what they reveal about what lies beneath the surface. This insight significantly expanded our thinking about accelerating learning.

I concluded that leaders in the Imagination Age (sometimes referred to as Industry 4.0 or the digital economy) need to up-scale their capabilities and resiliency as they take on more complex assignments and encounter more complex situations and problems in our increasingly hyper-connected world. A world where small changes propagate at network speeds leading to an even more contingent world that will tax all of their technical and mental capabilities. This understanding helped me set up the questions of how to address this on an enterprise level. My hypothesis was to create a culture of entrepreneurial resiliency where real world learning experiences help set the stage for our leaders to become true entrepreneurial learners, they must have a disposition that:

- Is always questioning, connecting, and probing
- Is deeply curious and listening to others
- Is always learning with and from others
- Is reading context as much as reading content
- Is continuously learning from interacting with the world, almost as if in conversation with the world
- Is willing to reflect on performance, alone and with the help of others — that is, becoming a **reflective practitioner**

To facilitate the accomplishment of building a culture of entrepreneurial learning that supports the reflective practitioner, we created the Fung Academy as a learning arm of the Fung Group (**www.funggroup. com**), a \$20B company that makes clothes, shoes, and accessories for brands and retailers and is often described as the world's leading supply chain orchestrator.

The Group is Hong Kong family lead, 114 years old, and participates in every stage of global business from sourcing, trading, logistics/distribution, to retail. Of note is we have maintained a spirit of "entrepreneurialism" as a key element of our culture and related business models.

The Academy was created to address three distinct learning challenges that form the basis of the capabilities needed to win in a networked, digitally enabled world. First, as a network orchestrator we operate an asset light model. That is, we do not own any of the 15,000 factories we utilize to make products; rather we orchestrate the production and distribution process for each order for our 2000 global customers. Second, on any given day, we will have 1–3 million workers spread across 40 geographies in Asia, India, and Africa involved in our production and distribution process. Third, in a Whitewater World, we clearly understood the network that learns fastest wins.

A Tribe of Entrepreneurial Learners — First Job of the Academy

We first needed to re-establish a culture of learning across the Group (we were able to go back 30 years when somehow it was built into our operating DNA). This would need to include leadership development through technical skills. Starting with context and Whitewater Principles (being careful to avoid building competency traps), we built a new leadership development process and coupled it to our innovation journey making significant strategic and organizational changes along the way. We accomplished this (it is ongoing and in a sense never ending) by developing an entirely new learning scaffolding (we partnered with Stanford and MIT) to gain a competitive edge through supporting a spirit of entrepreneurial learning that supported the capabilities required to be a reflective practitioner. We built innovation process/skills (e.g., design thinking, rapid prototyping) into the learning culture and turned the word failure (fail fast) into the word learning (learn fast).

Beyond Corporate Social Responsibility (CSR) — Sustainability as Competitive Advantage

We also understood that as a company we had a significant social responsibility to improve the lives of the workers in our factories, all of which are in emerging (with the exception of China) economies. To address this issue (Sustainability is a Fung Family value) we built a Supply Chain Futures unit into the Academy to work on making Sustainability an operating priority (including environmental and social compliance) in our 15,000 factories. Through a digitally driven learning platform we have pushed worker training along with health and finance learning to our factory base to improve economic conditions as well as avoid worker tragedies in Bangladesh and other emerging market economies where our production takes place (there is a Stanford Case study — "Everything is Connected" — written on these efforts). To finish this part of the narrative, we are turning the cost of sustainability into a competitive advantage through utilizing our learning/innovation processes to address environmental issues/social issues in our factories and their surrounding communities. Brands and retailers can then use this to show transparency and sustainable sourcing of their products to an increasingly socially concerned consumer.

Digitalization for Speed, Innovation, Transparency
We are bringing all this together as part of a significant enterprise transformation as we move from an analog to a digital world. First, by digitalizing our strategy enabled by the exponential increase in computing power and second turning our business model around — from just producing in the east and selling to the west to producing in the east and selling to both the west and the east thereby addressing the rise of consumption in Asia/Africa where 3.8 billion new consumers will be digitally connected by 2038. This 180-degree geographic turn, coupled with the volatility of the world we are shaping and simultaneously becoming a part of, has added significant urgency to resourcing and supporting our entrepreneurial learning environment that is growing reflective practitioners at digital speed.

Keywords
Global Strategy, Digital Economy, Entrepreneurial Learners, Sustainability

About the Author: Leonard Lane, DM
Dr. Lane is a Senior Lecturer at the Paul Merage School of Business, Member of the Board Fung Academy and Advisor to the Group Chairman Li & Fung Limited, Hong Kong. In this capacity, he advises the Group's businesses on how to take advantage of the exponential increases in technology to improve sustainable production and design as well as improve the lives of the 3–4 million people that work across the Group's global value chain.

Dr. Lane earned his BA in Political Science (1963) and his MBA (1968) from the University of Southern California and completed his Doctor of Management from Case Western Reserve University in 2003. He has held senior leadership positions in manufacturing and transportation orga-

nizations, run his own global consulting firm with offices in Anchorage, Seattle and Hong Kong, served in the U.S. Marine Corps and is a Hawaii Ironman finisher.

Gabriel Berczely

Because I was looking for an international and comprehensive academic experience, with a practical management approach, the DM program at the Weatherhead School of Management came out as the best alternative from several I analyzed, considering factors such as prestige, content, location, faculty, and cohort mix.

The Unexpected Returns from the Doctor of Management (DM) at the Weatherhead School of Management

I have been asked many times, by family, friends, and business colleagues, "Why a doctoral degree at your age?" I was 57 when I made the decision. If it were for teaching purposes, I was already adjunct professor and member of the Academic Council at the ESE Business School in Santiago, Chile. If it were for business reasons, a doctoral degree did not add too much value, if any at all, because the academic orientation of such a degree (intensive research and rigorous academic conclusions) is quite distant from the practical requirements of business life (fast and practical decision making, intuition based on experience and expertise).

Moreover, of course, the second question was, "Why at the Weatherhead School of Management?" Not only because the Management School of Case Western Reserve University (CWRU) is not known in Chile, but also because attending a doctoral program far away from home, which required one trip a month from Santiago to Cleveland for three years, sounded like an expensive and tiresome program with very little practical value and no evident return on investment.

Both questions were difficult to answer because any rational approach to them ended in a "does not make too much sense" remark. Nonetheless, as many things in life, emotional issues play a more important role than rational ones. In addition, to be frank, I never looked at this doctoral program as a monetary investment. It simply was a pending subject in my bucket list, and very coherent with one of my strong beliefs in life: "never get intellectually pensioned, constantly re-invent yourself."

Because I was looking for an international and comprehensive academic experience, with a practical management approach, the DM program at the Weatherhead School of Management came out as the best alternative from several I analyzed, considering factors such as prestige, content, location, faculty, and cohort mix. There is no doubt in my mind that this doctoral program went beyond any expectation I had when starting the journey.

First, the intellectual return was much bigger than I envisioned at the beginning, growing systematically, month after month, when confronted with different subjects lectured by excellent professors, discussions maintained with classmates and faculty, deep learning on previously unfamiliar matters, and the writing of many essays.

Second, the practical return I could derive from my doctoral thesis was far bigger than originally expected. When defining the "problems of practice" for my research, I selected a very challenging issue related to business sustainability. That is, how can we improve our capacity to anticipate strategic moves instead of just adapting and reacting to industry changes. My doctoral thesis, *Improving the Capacity for Strategic Anticipation — How Upstream, Downstream and Lateral Immersion Contribute to Strategic Renewal*, presented at the Academy of Management (AOM) Annual Meeting in Philadelphia in 2014, resulted in a great practical contribution to the way I am currently approaching strategic challenges at my various businesses.

Last but not least, and even more unexpected, was the practical benefit for two working outcomes I never imagined. One was related with the publication of columns and articles in Chilean media. The many essays, the research proposal, and the two doctoral research papers (qualitative and quantitative) constituted a perfect way to learn and solidify the ability to write articles and columns based on logical arguments, research based with empirical evidence, and a concise process.

The other unexpected practical result is related to a new line of activity, which I was able to develop after the DM program. This activity was to conduct a radio program ("Economic and Business Lighthouse" — Radio Agricultura FM 92.1, Faro Economía y Empresa), which has national coverage and high ratings airing every working day from 7:00

to 8:00 PM, a peak time for executives and business people returning home. Improvisation, combined with previous research on the matters to be discussed, is critical to make a program dynamic and helpful for the audience. Interviewing business people with semi-structured, open-ended questions during my qualitative research in the DM program improved my listening abilities, as well as the alertness required for further open-ended and intelligent questions.

For sure, CWRU's DM degree was tough and time-consuming, so that graduation was something similar to having conquered the peak of a very challenging mountain. However, every cent I spent, and every moment of my life I invested in this program, was not only fully worth it but also completely aligned with my aim to continuously reinvent myself. The residency based design of this doctoral degree, its content and approach, and the quality of the faculty and cohort were key elements for fun and the emotional and practical results generated by this fantastic three-year journey at the Weatherhead School of Management.

Keywords
Intellectual Return, Emotional Return, Lifelong Learning, Doctoral Program, Adult Education, Practitioner Research, Strategic Anticipation

About the Author: Gabriel Berczely, DM
Dr. Berczely is a serial entrepreneur that owns businesses in a variety of industries. He is Chairman and/or member of several boards and two foundations, Adjunct Professor of Strategy at the ESE Business School in Chile, member of its Academic Committee since 2000 and fellow of the International Academy of Management. Dr. Berczely writes weekly columns in the digital daily El Libero in Santiago, and co-conducts a daily radio program from 7:00 to 8:00 PM (Faro Economia y Negocio, Radio Agricultura 92.1) with national coverage.

Deirdre Dixon

Now I understand how to best learn from my experiences and help others do the same, and link it to theory, which is powerful. Learning how to learn, and how to investigate and combine those into teaching was not something I was expecting to receive from the program.

In Extremis Story

I will be honest and blunt; I went to Case Western Reserve University to get the letters behind my name. As a teacher, I was ignorant enough to not know what I did not know, and — at the time — I really did not think I needed additional schooling in order to do my teaching job well. However, wiser, more experienced people told me that an advanced degree was necessary to be successful in the academic world. I started this process needing to "punch a ticket" but I quickly realized just how valuable the education and training offered by the Doctor of Management (DM) programs at Case Western Reserve University (CWRU) is in the world. The degree offered by CWRU allowed me to impact the world. Let me start from the beginning.

My life's mission has always been service. In high school, besides being involved with sports, I was a Girl Scout, volunteered with the Red Cross, taught Sunday school, and did other volunteer work. When I started contributing, my objective was to serve others. As I have matured, I realized that my initial, personal goal could be compounded and expanded by helping others achieve *their* goals in better and more effective ways. In this way, my goal for the past decade or so has been to serve others so that people can become better leaders and help make the world a better place.

My personal contribution is my service to others, but my impact — expanded through my training and education — is helping people become better leaders. I have done this in several phases of my life. In the military, I helped those around me, especially those who worked for me, improve their leadership through role modeling, mentoring, and authentic leadership. Once I retired, I started working in executive education with a specialty in leadership. Now, as a tenure track professor, I help teach students, both undergraduates and graduates, about leadership. I still do this through role modeling, mentoring, and authentic leadership. I served in the Army and now I serve my students. In addition, as I have served, I have learned that helping others learn about being better leaders through my own experience and research on leadership expands and grows my impact.

I retired from the Army after 20 years, and I began teaching and working in the Center for Leadership at the University of Tampa. I had many duties in this job, but I loved teaching the most. Having been a practitioner for over 20 years, I was using my experience to teach the lessons I had learned the hard way. It was a win-win for me and for my students.

However, after about three years of part-time teaching, the Dean of the College of Business at my school suggested I get an advanced degree so I could teach full time. I was not really convinced I needed an advanced degree, because I was already teaching, and my students loved my content. Despite my reservations regarding the time, expense, and additional commitment, I decided to look into it because I was interested in teaching full time. My attitude was that I needed to get the advanced degree in order to teach, but I really knew everything I needed to know about teaching. Boy was that wrong. However, as I said, sometimes, you do not know what you do not know.

Nevertheless, what I did know was that a good school, one that was reputable and solid with its experience, was important. My family calls me a school snob, but my reasoning is that the reputation of your school matters. I want to learn from the best and I want to be challenged. Therefore, I searched long and hard for a doctoral program that fit me. I knew a few things: I wanted it to be an Association to Advance Collegiate Schools of Business (AACSB) accredited school, I wanted to be with students like me, not 20 somethings, I wanted the school to have a good reputation, and, finally, I did not want to take six years to complete the program. I checked several schools around me first, but all of them said the average time to complete a degree was six to seven years. That was unacceptable to me. I wanted to have the most impact as soon as possible.

I also knew I needed a great deal of expertise about research. I needed experts to teach me and that knowledge focused me on CWRU since it was a top tier research university. I have always had immense pride in the universities I have attended. I went to the United States Military Academy for my undergraduate and Duke University for my MBA. It made sense that I wanted my terminal degree to be from a school with a great standing.

I came into the DM program knowing what I wanted to study. When I was in Iraq, as an officer in charge of a company of over 200 soldiers, I remembered sitting around talking to people about why some leaders were successful and some were not. This was personal to me. Lives were at stake — both then and now. I was interested in what made these leaders in these dangerous environments effective, and how I could help my soldiers and others improve before they even landed in a country. That is what I wanted to investigate. I wanted to make a difference with my research and help others, specifically those who would be going into dangerous environments. Once in the

> **The program taught me how to research and how to investigate problems. I came to understand that a PhD was just the beginning.**

program, I got so involved in my research that I decided to stay and do the PhD program so I could continue my research. What I realized in my time at this great school, however, was that this was just the start of my research, not the end!

My problem of practice was a good one, and I was excited to learn about what makes leaders in *in extremis* Army situations successful. What I did not expect was how much I learned about teaching and research and how to be a better leader myself. I learned not just about my subject, but I learned about learning and about research. Even as a lifelong learner, I still did not understand how much I had to discover. The program taught me how to research and how to investigate problems. I came to understand that a PhD was just the beginning.

My research has taken me unexpected places, geographically and intellectually. My dissertation was on leaders *in extremis*, or leaders in dangerous situations. I began with Army soldiers. I did a qualitative study of 30 Army leaders who had recently returned from the Middle East (Dixon, Weeks, Boland, & Perelli, 2016). I based much of that research around Weick's (1995) sense-making. That qualitative study lead me to do a survey which I expanded to all military (Dixon, Boland, Weeks, & Gaskin, 2015). The military study illustrated that the most successful leaders in these perilous environments were leaders that had mental flexibility, a sense of duty, and that they had self-esteem.

> **The training I received at CWRU has helped me to become a better teacher, and a better leader. That is the highest compliment I could give of any program.**

After these interesting results, I wanted to learn about leaders in other dangerous environments. I expanded my mixed-method study into a survey in other *in extremis* contexts of fire fighters and law enforcement personnel, looking at both situational awareness (Endsley, 1995) and self efficacy (Chen, Gully, & Eden, 2001). The most interesting thing from that study was the finding that one cannot look at all *in extremis* leaders as the same: the reason they go into the dangerous context matters. For firefighters and law enforcement, they enter the environment to help strangers. For military members, the soldiers and other military personal are usually fighting for one another (Dixon, 2014).

Because of my *in extremis* work, I have been invited by the Navy to participate in a research project with Navy SEALS, trying to help discover what makes a person successful in completing the difficult training. Hardiness, resilience, ethical mindset, grit, and physical bio markers are just a few of the constructs we are examining. This research hopes to mitigate the large dropout rate of the SEAL training through learning what can make individuals successful before they enter the initial training. Our team is working with the Joint Special Operations University and the Department of the Navy, who have provided funding and access for our research team to conduct the research in California where the training occurs.

I am an associate Director in the TECO Energy Center for Leadership at the University of Tampa. In this job, I have become one of the leadership experts at my university. When one of my colleagues is doing a research project that encompasses leadership, they often seek me out. I have co-authored several articles on entrepreneurship with other professors where they have asked me to provide the leadership angle of the paper. I co-authored a case study on entrepreneurship published in *Entrepreneurship Education and Pedagogy* on restaurants (Dixon, Miscuraca, & Koutroumanis, 2018). The journal said it was the third most downloaded article in 2018.

Because of this leadership area of interest and expertise, one of my latest research forays is examining women farmers in Kenya, specifically how their leadership identity changes when they are given land. The research began about entrepreneurship and once my colleagues began to interview the women, they realized it was also about leadership identity. I was able to come onto the project and add the leadership lens. Our first presentation on this research was at a conference in China (Pennington, Salin, & Dixon, 2019).

I am still doing this research on leaders in dangerous environments today, and it has expanded in wonderful ways. I received a grant to study Rhinoceros horn conservation in South Africa, Botswana, and Swaziland, and I am returning to southern Africa for the second year to collect additional information on how leaders in the dangerous environment of the world of rhino poaching can make a difference in rhino conservation. The research question is about how leaders at a local level can make a difference in the rhino horn conservation issues. The black market for rhino horn products in areas such as Vietnam and China has driven the price so high that poachers are willing to risk everything to obtain the horn (Hanks, 2015). In turn, the rangers and park guides are willing to risk their lives to save the dwindling rhino population. In addition, the different countries have different leadership approaches to solving their problems. Each country has slightly different rules for Rhino protection. For example, Swaziland has a shoot to kill poachers on sight policy, while South Africa has a more tolerant policy for rangers with poachers. For this research project I have interviewed park rangers, field guides, local college students studying wildlife, and native peoples of the area to name a few. The main thing I have learned so far is that this situation is not as black and white as it may seem, but what remains the same is that leadership in solving problems matters.

What I am really trying to accomplish, across all of these research projects, is helping others become better leaders, which leads to social change in a myriad of environmental contexts. If individuals can learn to be better leaders, they are better problem solvers, and no matter what amount of authority they may have, all of society benefits. Improving leadership leads to improvement across all cultural, geographical, and economic boundaries, as evidenced by my studies in the United States, Iraq, Africa, and China. Understanding human behavior and decision-making, and especially in perilous situations, helps everyone. I am making a difference in the world by helping individuals improve their leadership and helping to solve global societal problems.

Competent leaders at every level can make a difference. When I teach leadership, I always start with the individual. You have to know yourself first and then learn about others. Followership is an important part of leadership. My goal is to have every student comprehend that they must know themselves, be a good follower, then start being a leader.

All these opportunities were opened to me because of learning how to research at CWRU and following my passion for leadership. Research was not the primary reason I was drawn to CWRU, I just wanted to earn my PhD so I could teach. However, as I learned, my teaching, much to my initial surprise, improved. I had had 20 years of leadership experience and I thought that that was enough. I learned that understanding your subject from an academic point of view does matter.

Prior to the program, I was teaching based only on my limited, personal experience. Sometimes I did not have a thorough understanding of why things worked the way they did, or why certain leaders were successful. I then learned how to teach integrating both experience and theoretical underpinnings. Now I understand how to best learn from my experiences and help others do the same, and link it to theory, which is powerful. Learning how to learn, and how to investigate and combine those into teaching was not something I was expecting to receive from the program. Now I cannot imagine my life without it.

The value of the CWRU DM Programs is still that they are a valued AACSB accredited program that teaches individuals how to excel in research, but it is so much more than that. One will also gain lifelong friends. Connecting with people is an area I was not expecting to gain from a PhD program. The cohort program is a strong one, and I still keep in close contact with more than a handful of students in my class. We have even gone on vacation together! We occasionally do research together, meet up at conferences, and just check in on one another for birthdays, etc. We were a strong team that helped one another through the program and our relationships have only strengthened through the years. The relationships I formed while at CWRU were just an added bonus; I certainly was not thinking about that when I picked my PhD program!

I am often asked what I miss about the Army when I retired. I usually say two things, "making a difference every day" and "the people." Now I realize when I teach, I am still making a difference, just to a different audience. I have been teaching for over 20 years, and I received my PhD five years ago. I go up for tenure next year. My pre-tenure packet was above expectations in both scholarship and service and meets expectations in teaching. My marks in both scholarship and teaching are from what I learned at CWRU. The professors there taught me how to question, and how to find answers, and I continue to do that today. The people I met in the program helped expand my personal experience and knowledge, and I am a better leader because of them and because of this program. Last year I received the Dean's award for excellence in teaching. The training I received at CWRU has helped me to become a better teacher, and a better leader. That is the highest compliment I could give of any program.

Keywords

Service to Others, Leaders in *In Extremis*, Teaching Leadership

About the Author: Deirdre Dixon, PhD

After spending 22 years as an Army officer with experience in Iraq, Dr. Dixon decided to apply her knowledge and practical leadership experience to teaching and designing leadership programs. Dr. Dixon is currently at the University of Tampa. She is a graduate of West Point, earned her MBA from Duke, and her PhD from Case Western Reserve University. Her area of research interest is in extremis leadership.

James R. Hemsath

Ageism is a sneaky thing and shows up in many ways; fortunately, the DM program did not care and that was what was so powerful about the program — the interest is in your mind and your ideas and that example is transformational in its own right. The approach to relevance and rigor and finding "Research that Matters" was critical to me.

A Story of Fate, of Transition, and What to Do When I Grow Up

The dream of having a doctorate has been one that was long on the horizon. I had completed a second Master's degree at the University of Alaska as a demonstration that in my late 40's I still had the capacity to work at an academic level. I also did so with the intent that I would continue with my PhD in Engineering Management, and in particular Project Management, across different cultures. When I reached 60, I was being pressed to answer the question of what do I want to do when I retire? To me, this was a non-question, why would I want to retire. After all, retirement is just another word for unemployment. Pressed to articulate a little better, I created a 2x2 matrix that talked about travel, fitness, hobbies, the desire to understand research, and how development could take place in the Arctic. My goal was to use scenarios and system dynamics to look at this area. I put this matrix in my "to do someday" file and in that file was an ad from *Harvard Business Review*, complete with student testimony, about the Case Western Reserve University (CWRU) Doctor of Management (DM) program. Ironically, I cannot find that ad to be able to tell that particular DM'er that they helped change my life.

As a former Clevelander, I was well familiar with CWRU and Weatherhead School of Management and resonated with the concept of the practitioner scholar and bridging from the scholarly world to the application world. I was not, at this point of my life, necessarily interested in a transitioning to academia, but more interested in two things: making a difference in the Arctic and learning new things. The DM program was highly focused on these two concepts. Of course, once I embarked on this next journey the questions changed to why do you want to do this (… at your age), how can this help your career (… at your age), what possible benefit could there be for you (… at your age)? Ageism is a sneaky thing and shows up in many ways; fortunately, the DM program did not care and that was what was so powerful about the program — the interest is in your mind and your ideas and that example is transformational in its own right. The approach to relevance and rigor and finding "Research that Matters" was critical to me.

My research did focus on that original retirement goal about how do we get things done in the Arctic, specifically how can people work together coming from different places and cultures. This is on a moving scale from outright conflict to competition, with only winners and losers to cooperation, on a negotiated solution, to collaboration where new and innovative approaches can be found. This need for multi-party transnational collaboration is key to achieving things in a complex environment. My work produced a number of findings that are applicable now, specifically: 1) Understanding, organizing and managing for cultural differences is a go/no go process — if you do not lead, manage, train, and plan for those different cultures you will not get through the gate, but once you are through cultural awareness training alone will not guarantee collaboration; 2) In this environment, getting people, the team, to relate or connect is key and is based on empathy and trust. Empathy is first on the list and focuses on understanding the other parties' constraints, expectations, and needs — not just feelings; 3) Without trust there will be no collaboration. You are trusted or not and it can be lost in a moment. Trust is earned and is built on experience; it is based on action and it takes time and that time must be built into the process; and 4) The creation of a fused identity is the outcome of empathy and trust. A fused identity is the result of individual identities coming together in the context of the team and project — parent, engineer, environmentalist, project manager — where your identity is not lost and your voice is heard; (5) The ability to adapt and continue to refine your vision, one that morphs and grows from the collective view as you learn more about your universe is key to any complex system or wicked problem which work in the Arctic surely is. Rather than a shared vision an *adaptive shared vision* is key. This requires an iterative approach, eating the elephant one bite at a time, which interestingly enough provides the time needed to build trust, learn about each other through empathy, and along the road create a fused identity. It is a system with the goal of true collaboration.

For me, the motivation of obtaining a doctorate was never vocational; it was always about the learning and the research. However, change continues unabated. Retiring at 65 was not in my plans; I anticipated working much longer than that so the need for some vocational opportunities has gained more importance for me. I am on a number of boards – Alaska Aerospace Corporation, North Slope Science Initiative, the UAA College of Engineering Advisory Board, and a subcommittee for the Arctic Research Consortium US (ARCUS), all made possible in part by experience but in no small part by having that Doctorate. All of these are a start. As a direct result of my doctorate (and relations with the University), I am currently teaching a class in Organizational Behavior in the College of Business and Public Policy at the University of Alaska Anchorage utilizing much of what I have learned at Weatherhead. This is an adjunct position and in the next semester, I will continue to teach OB and will add a class on the Applications of Management. It has been suggested that I could possibly receive an appointment as an Assistant Professor at the college in the fall of 2020.

> **For me, the motivation of obtaining a doctorate was never vocational; it was always about the learning and the research.**

I have also had the opportunity to share my research at a number of conferences — the PMI Global Congress (2017), University of the Arctic Congress (2018), Arctic Frontiers 2019 (abstracts accepted but I was unable to present), and at the Arctic Futures 2050 Conference at the National Academy of Science in the fall of 2019. This latter conference is important to note. Arctic Futures 2050 was organized around key panel sessions and poster sessions. I was fortunate enough to be selected to have a poster displayed — a lone management poster in a sea of science — but what is important was the interaction on the panels. There was obvious discord between the indigenous peoples of the Arctic and the variety of researchers that are investigating climate change and other Arctic science issues. The tension between indigenous/ traditional knowledge and western scientific knowledge was palpable. All at a time when everyone is clamoring for collaboration and collaborative research, yet in my scale these folks are not collaborating, they are barely cooperating and the relationships are degrading to conflict. The best comment was researchers are like Snow Geese: everyone in the community knows when they will show up, they will eat everything in sight, crap over everything, and when winter comes, they will leave. The root cause of this tension — a complete lack of trust. In my research world on collaboration, trust is understood to be the grease that lets things get done, yet the creation of that trust is somewhat a mystery. *This is a big deal* and unless addressed will impede not only the necessary research into changes in the Arctic that Climate Change has brought but will impact the ability to take any of the actions necessary to allow our indigenous Arctic communities to survive.

I have begun the early conversations about how "I" might be able to conduct a research program into the establishment of trust in these communities to assure that both science and engineering can take place in the Arctic. What is ironic is that if a sequential mixed methods approach of grounded theory and quantitative analysis had been followed, the traditional knowledge (lived experiences) would have been part of the larger conversation and the tension in place would not have developed at all or would have been minimized. Research into trust in these situations will be delicate and the first order of business must be the development of a collaborative approach with Arctic indigenous leaders. I envision a mixed methods approach utilizing interviews, a nominal group technique, and/or action research approach in conjunction with a Delphi technique (i.e., communication with panels of experts). The goal will be to create a proposal for funding by the National Science Foundation Arctic Research program. The product of this research is interesting. First, is the development of a process that can be utilized by agencies and organizations doing research in the Arctic. Second, the very process of the research program has the ability to develop trust and be a case study for

Having participated in the DM Program has given me a new viewpoint to see the world and to continue the research that I started.

collaborative Arctic research as well as for the execution of the necessary projects that must be executed to save the Arctic for the people of the Arctic. Finally the creation of a teaching case study on building trust. This is a time critical opportunity to make a significant difference in the lives of many, many people in the Arctic.

Prior to this "epiphany" and potential research opportunity on trust, my DM research had pointed to the need to understand better what an iterative adaptive shared vision is. Research is needed on this subject and my goal is to continue my research investigating the phenomenon of maintaining the motivation of the collective vision that brought people together while adapting that vision as new information becomes available. At this point, I envision looking through the lens of boundary spanning where each representative of a "party" that makes up the multiparty "team" has to span their organization with the variety of Expectations, Constraints, Cultures, Identities, and Motivations. This spanning occurs in two different dimensions — one through the individual organization and the second the team itself.

My journey at Weatherhead began with half a sheet of paper where I had written that I wanted to do in the next phase of my life. I identified teaching and research as being important and that lead me to CWRU. I thought that I would get my degree and then I would just "do". I never envisioned that this would mean that I would be learning for the rest of my life. Additionally, it's not just research that drives me. Inspired by work done in courses on designing sustainable systems, understanding complex systems and on sustainability and social value creation, I have written up a proposal for a book looking to identify sentinels for change, both human and biologic, that point to aspects of climate change where local action must be taken. There is a completely new field to get my arms around to do this, but if I am successful, this book could also lead to making a difference in the Arctic.

At graduation, my mother asked me if getting the doctorate was everything I imagined. I told her it was and more. As an aside, I am not sure that my mom truly understood why I was doing this; just that I was excited and came to Cleveland once a month so we could visit. I had the chance to bring Mom to campus a couple of times and she had a chance to meet both faculty and staff. That aside done, every class I took was applicable to what I was doing at the time. My experience in part inspired both one of my project managers and my son to tackle a Master's degree in executive style programs. The new world that I was introduced to was larger than I ever imagined, the concept of research truly was transformational and I have become a research junkie. Having participated in the DM Program has given me a new viewpoint to see the world and to continue the research that I started. To paraphrase Spiderman, with great powers come great responsibilities and I both feel and carry the responsibility of having a DM from the Weatherhead School of Management.

Keywords
Collaboration, Transformation, Trust, Research, Arctic

About the Author: James Hemsath, DM
Dr. Hemsath has over 40 years of experience managing large projects and economic development in the Arctic. This work encompassed the public sector (State of Alaska) as well as the private sector. Private sector experience includes managing large projects, predominately in the oil and gas fields. As a member of the U.S. Department of Energy's Arctic Energy Office, he managed research projects at the University of Alaska Fairbanks. As a Senior Fellow at the Institute of the North, he developed and led an International Polar Year project on Arctic Energy. Dr. Hemsath was a recipient of a NASA Faculty Fellowship at Kennedy Space Center. Currently retired, he works part time as an adjunct professor teaching organizational behavior as well as consulting on Arctic energy issues.

"*There is never a chance that we will run out of things to explore.*"

Sylvia Earle

Explorer

Becoming curious about the surrounding environment and individual self and uses that curiosity to shape the environment

Jeff Ferguson

I saw the DM Program as a means to broaden my thinking, gain a better, deeper understanding of organizational dynamics, and become a better decision-maker as a business practitioner.

Reflections of the DM Program

It has been 20 years since I graduated from the Doctor of Management (DM) program at Case Western Reserve University (CWRU). I was a member of the second cohort. Challenging, enervating, exhausting, stressful, and stimulating are words that best describe the experience. Without question, it was personally transformative in a variety of ways. However, I believe that a large part of this transformation occurred because for both myself and many of my fellow classmates, we were at a point in our careers where we were ready for change. For some, it may have been perceived as an opportunity to advance their career. For other cohort members, it could have been a recognition that we were becoming stale in our thinking and had begun to view organizational issues with the same tried, tired, and previously attempted solutions. We may have been losing some creative thinking to developing solutions. Most of all, however; I think that we were open to change ourselves, our jobs, and the manner in which we viewed issues whether the issues were internal to our current organizations or were more global pertaining to wider societal concerns. I saw the DM Program as a means to broaden my thinking, gain a better, deeper understanding of organizational dynamics, and become a better decision-maker as a business practitioner. I believe that the program transformed me in three main ways.

Personal Capacity

The first change actually occurred very early in the program. It involved gaining a better understanding of myself and my own capacity for juggling and handling significant responsibilities simultaneously. I worked full-time throughout the program. I held responsibilities for managing several hundred million dollars of revenue for senior care facilities in nine states. Unfortunately, the states were not contiguous; half were on the west coast while the others were in the Midwest. I traveled a lot, usually three to four days every week. Once the program started, I never went anywhere without books, syllabi, and a computer. I quickly learned that every day would be devoted to a bracket of time that would be broken into chunks — business, DM, and family. With a mid-evening 20-minute nap, I disciplined myself to four and a half hours of sleep each night. Two of our three sons were in college at the time. The youngest was in high school. Candidly, I could not have done the DM program if the two older boys were still in high school. Their activities and events kept my wife and I busy attending and participating with them in their lives.

> **Through the DM program, I looked for books and articles that were more philosophical, ones that made me think about an issue rather than merely read about or recite what a certain CEO had done to fix a problem.**

I used vacation days to attend the Friday residences. I lived in Perrysburg, Ohio during the program. Fortunately, I had a friend in the program as a classmate who lived very close. We met at 6:00 AM on Fridays and drove to Cleveland for the weekend residences. She had a friend whom she stayed with on Friday nights while I had a brother who I stayed with overnight. The benefit of our shared commute was an opportunity to discuss the weekend ahead of us and to decompress at the weekend's completion.

After the first residency, I found myself thinking, "I'm not sure I can handle all of this without something suffering". No one else in my company was trying to complete a doctorate while working full-time and no one, neither the CEO nor the COO, were going to cut me any slack just because I had decided to do this. I knew that I had their emotional support, but I still had to perform in my job. Once I decided to do whatever it took to keep all of the balls in the air at once, I found that I was ready to get on with each: the job, the school challenge, and the family. As Herbert Simon would have said, I probably did not maximize my ability in any one area, but "satisficing" got me through.

Making Complexity Understandable

Many of our class readings and discussions revolved around dealing with complex issues — organizational, societal, and, at times, personal. As a business leader who had to take complex issues, turn them into understandable terms, and then create actionable steps for managers to follow and execute on, I knew that I had to develop something. I worked with and led a group of managers who largely came from the caring disciplines — social work, ministry, nursing, or other health care backgrounds. For many, business terms were foreign. I might as well have been speaking German to many of the compassionate people who bore significant financial responsibilities. This chasm required the development of some type of understandable means or tool for running the business. Our class discussions dwelled on similar situations but in a different context. Using these discussions and white board examples as a model, I developed what I called "*The Five Key Success Factors for Running the Business*". I introduced this first to the Regional Managers who reported to me and then to the individual site managers. When I went to Marriott to lead their senior care business, I took the five keys with me and made them permeate the business unit. The five keys simplified what individual managers and leaders had to do in order to run a successful business. They provided focus, direction, and simplicity in a business that encompassed a great deal of complexity and emotion.

The five keys were as follows:

1. A commitment to quality of care and service
2. Look for ways to grow the revenue base
3. Control expenses
4. Collect your receivables to manage the cash for the business
5. Have the "right" people doing the "right" things at the "right" time with the "right" people

Each of the five points included a set of metrics, which measured performance for the given area. I also knew that merely initiating a program is not and would not be enough. There must be follow-up and follow-through in order to have it succeed. Each month I held a company-wide conference call for all managers where I recognized success stories in each area from different facilities so that everyone could see that if something was done well, they could and would, be commended for it while the entire organization listened. When annual budgets were developed, they were developed around the five keys. Facility strategic plans focused on how and where and when specific areas were to be addressed at the local level. The corporate plan utilized the same methodology to present the business direction to the parent organization. I knew that the "Five Keys" had been integrated into the organization when individual site managers and department heads could recite to me where they were, and what they were doing to attain success in their particular areas of responsibility. Without question, the utilization and implementation of the "Five Keys" enabled our team to improve the business' performance, which ultimately lead to the sale of the business to Sunrise Senior Living Services. I published the story of what we did with "The Five Keys" in *Senior Housing and Care Journal*. It was given the industry GE Award for Best Operating Practices. I believe that by developing and using the five Keys, we were able to build enthusiasm, increase energy, and ultimately improve financial performance faster than would have otherwise occurred without them. Much like a coach develops a game plan to execute upon; the five Keys provided a simplified game plan that made a complex business more understandable and focused for the operators.

Reflections

During the program's first year, we were required to write a reflection paper after each residency. This provided an opportunity to think about what we discussed, learned, or found undone from the weekend. We shared these reflections with each other. The reflection papers added to our learning. Each of us brought our own perspectives and experience lenses to the program. Many times, we interpreted the same events very differently. This highlighted how and why so many issues and occurrences in our society possess such widely varying opinions. I carried this exercise with me in each organization that I lead after the DM program. Monthly reviews made quarterly reviews easier to compile. In turn, the quarterly reviews made for handy references for an annual statement of what was accomplished and for establishing goals for the forthcoming year. Even though I had always been an introspective person, these reflection papers were habit-forming and easily adapted in the work world.

When Marriott decided to exit the industry, The American Senior Housing Association asked me to speak to company leaders as to the reasons and decisions that lead to this conclusion. I used this time as an opportunity to discuss this decision's ramifications for the entire senior living business. This would require a new cadre of leaders to step forward and serve as the benchmark for others. I titled this speech, "When a Great Company Exits a Business". Ultimately, this was reprinted in several industry trade journals.

Another side benefit of the reflections piece was how it changed my recreational reading. I had always read a lot, but it was mostly "how-to" business books and periodicals. Through the DM program, I looked for books and articles that were more philosophical, ones that made me think about an issue rather than merely read about or recite what a certain CEO had done to fix a problem. I became more interested in understanding the underlying issues and underpinnings of a problem and not just the steps taken to address it on the surface.

My advanced research project provided me with a different kind of reflection. I did a qualitative approach as to how regional managers (e.g., middle managers) in the long-term health care business dealt with stress. The interviews of 20 current and former regional managers demonstrated how many personal and intense events that occurred "under their watch" stayed with them. The organizations tended to provide support for patients, families, and other staff but did little, if anything, to assist the regional manager in processing through what were often tragic events. One of my conclusions was that companies, whether for-profit or not-for-profit, needed to do more to help these important people work through the mental issues that stuck with them. It was no wonder that the burnout for these jobs was so high. As I became a leader of organizations, I knew that a regional manager needed more training and support than they were normally given, and I tried to do so. Had I not done this research, I would not have had such strong personal insights into the life and trauma that many regionals dealt with and carried with them.

Whenever a business or organization makes a large investment, it recaps the investment and reviews its perceived success or failure, analyzes the results and assesses whether it was worth it or not. Education is a major investment in yourself, especially when it occurs after a number of "real" world experiences. You commit time and substantial dollars to it while making substantial trade-offs in both. A mid-career investment like the DM program requires that you ask whether you will obtain enough utility from the program to apply concepts and discussions to day-to-day challenges. Alternatively, will it be so theoretical that it will have little, if any, applications to work responsibilities? At least in my case, I saw its relevance. Perhaps I made it relevant to justify the investment in my own mind. My career changed dramatically after the DM program. Was it because I added another degree to my resume or was it because I became a more value-added executive because of what I learned from the program itself, its excellent faculty and my fellow classmates. Perhaps my career changes came about from a combination of both.

Keywords
Transformative, Capacity, Complexity, Reflection, Investment

About the Author: Jeff Ferguson, DM
Dr. Ferguson is a retired business executive living in Chestertown, Maryland. While enrolled in the DM Program he was Vice President of the Midwest Division for HCR/ManorCare. Shortly after receiving the DM degree, he became the CEO of Marriott Senior Living Services, which comprised 156 facilities in 32 states with annual revenues of more than $900m. Upon its sale to Sunrise Senior Living, he served as President of Operations for Erickson Retirement Communities. Later, he became the President/CEO of Sentient Medical Systems, a telemedicine company specializing in inter-operative monitoring of neurological and orthopedic surgeries.

Dr. Ferguson taught Business Management and Ethics in the Management Department of Anne Arundel Community College for several years as an Adjunct Professor. Active in community organizations, he served on the Planning Advisory Board for Anne Arundel County, which reviews and evaluates capital spending for the county and recommends actions for the County Executive. He also served on the Board of Directors for Annapolis Life Care, LLC. This included several years as Vice Presi-

dent and then President of the Board. Currently he serves on the state P-20 Leadership Council on Education where he chairs the committee to improve both adult GED preparation and passing rates.

Charles T. Moses

The research skills we mastered in the program have continued to serve me well, though I am these days more focused on developing policies and interventions, which address questions similar to those I researched as an EDM student.

My Academic Journey

One of the most powerful learning experiences of my life happened very early in what was then called the Executive Doctor of Management (EDM) program. Everyone in my cohort was trying to understand what doctoral level research was and made an initial stab at framing their own research question. Dr. Mohan Reddy told us that we should strive for generalizability: good research should have some relevance for someone other than ourselves. "The question is who does your research have meaning for...and why?" he told us.

That has been the standard that I have tried to use in my research since hearing those words in 2001. It was also the beginning of a journey, from teaching and research to higher education administration. As a dean, I do not publish as much research as I did as a faculty member. My thinking on the concepts I explored in the DM program has certainly evolved. Yet I act on those questions differently. I am more practitioner than scholar these days.

It was in those early DM seminars that I developed my research question: "Why do some groups, lacking money but possessing rich social networks, enjoy a more robust economic life than others having more money, but fewer "ties"?

As I wrote in my dissertation:

Networks are a powerful, yet confounding, dimension of socio-economic life. When strong and insular, they can be good for a community, providing rich material rewards, information, and validation. In the extreme, these same networks can become parochial and nepotistic, closed to all but the initiated and the elite, breeding grounds for rent seeking and economic inefficiency. Conversely, when networks are excessively diffuse and porous, they leave a community with little economic purchase: business and money flow with few lasting benefits to the polity. (Moses 2004, p. 1)

My research led me to various theories related to social capital and economic development. Among the prominent researchers in this area was Putnam (2000). I also read the literature on locus of control (Rotter et al., 1966) which focused on why groups are internally or externally focused.

The three research projects that I did over the course of the DM program focused on the economic challenges faced by developing communities. My first-year project, "Newtown Stationery: Getting Communities back into the Economic Development Game," is an ethnographic study of the experiences of a single entrepreneur and explores issues of bridging (external) and bonding (internal) in an inner city setting. The main figure in this study was "Ms. C.", founder of a stationery store on one of the busiest streets in the neighborhood. Ms. C's struggles to find operating capital for her business and the bridging networks. She was able to access via contacts outside of the community illustrate the power of social networks.

The second-year project, "Inner City Economic Empowerment: A Tale of Two Cities," was a study of the dynamics of economic development in the predominately African American business communities of Durham and Charlotte, North Carolina. Using social capital theory, the project utilized a larger sample to develop constructs and a deeper understanding of the relationship between networks and economic development. I used qualitative methodology to try to make sense of the rich descriptions of the challenges faced by African American entrepreneurs in both cities. The research questions for the project were:

- What constructs do respondents say are factors in generating economic development?
- How do inner city entrepreneurs evaluate the effectiveness of government interventions and locally driven modalities purporting to serve them?
- What kinds of networks and structures result from the social, political and historical relationships in the inner city?
- What kinds of outcomes are most often perceived to be efficacious to inner city development?

Interviews were conducted with 19 entrepreneurs in both cities. Qualitative coding techniques were employed to develop common themes and to set the stage for my third-year research project.

The third-year project, "Entrepreneurial Emergence: Key Congruence Factors and Community Processes," detailed how networks and orientation (defined as locus-of-control) increase the level of profitable and sustainable businesses in a community. The main conclusion of the project is that there needs to be a better alignment between the economic needs of the community and the government intervention designed to help. Other findings supported the idea that both bridging and bonding networks are important for entrepreneurial emergence.

My ultimate aim in pursuing the three projects was to provide those involved in the design and implementation of community-based entrepreneurial assistance programs with another framework for understanding how best to build programs that leverage extant community assets to maximally empower local businesspeople and residents. This is a variation on what some have characterized as the "Third Wave" of capitalism, which extolls the virtues of market-based approaches to community economic development but says little about the way in which these crowd out nascent businesses in struggling communities. "The answer to poverty is capitalism" (Jacoby & Siegel, 1999, p. 22). "Not government handouts but private business. Corporations would tap into a forgotten pool of workers, while mainstream investors and indigenous entrepreneurs would create a local economy that edged out ghetto culture" (p. 22).

Sen (1999) expounds on the point: "It is hard to think that any process of substantial development can do without very extensive use of markets. But that does not preclude the role of social support and public regulations... when they can enrich — rather than impoverish — human lives" (p. 7).

Economic development in minority communities of that era was often a heroic act. Founders usually started with little money and no avenue to formal financing. They often found themselves at the mercy of a hostile political and economic establishment. Government programs designed to help often-fostered displacement. The improving economic conditions in some communities put commercial rents out of reach for the companies they were designed to help. I used the ideas of Foucault and Derrida, two postmodernist philosophers, to ground this idea. "Derrida's conception of deconstruction and Foucault's analysis of power suggested a particular type of postmodern politics — one rooted in local, often personal acts of resistance against the constraints of discursive structures rooted in "false" claims of truth... marginalized individuals could be empowered by waging struggles against the totalizing systems of knowledge/power on the local level and re-creating their individual identities ways that did not conform to dominant ideologies" (Gumming, 1998, p. 477).

> The concepts that we discussed in the EDM program helped me to form a research agenda that carried into my first formal academic assignment as a tenure-track assistant professor of management at Clark Atlanta University.

Ms. C. is one example of what a determined entrepreneur, well anchored in a community, can accomplish. "… Social scientists offer truncated social networks and inadequate social skills as an important part of the explanation for perpetual poverty," Jackson, 2001, p. 122). However, he adds, "... the lack of such advancement is not reducible to the idea that there are no such networks at all" (p. 122).

The concepts that we discussed in the DM program helped me to form a research agenda that carried into my first formal academic assignment as a tenure-track assistant professor of management at Clark Atlanta University. In 2007, I co-authored my first peer review journal article: "Internationalizing the Business Faculty via an International Spring Tour: Implications for AACSB Accredited Historically Black College and University Business Programs." The article focused on the international immersion programs at a group of historically black colleges in the United States.

In the years since, I have published 10 articles in peer-reviewed journals. The research skills we mastered in the program have continued to serve me well, though I am these days more focused on developing policies and interventions, which address questions similar to those I researched as an DM student.

The University of San Francisco (USF) is a medium-sized, Jesuit university located in one of America's most dynamic cities. USF's core values include "Social Justice" and "Conscious Capitalism." Its business school faculty teach classes incorporating Ignatian values and ethics and management practices and there is a lot of discussion within the school about the Business Roundtables' recent statement bringing all "stakeholders" into greater focus. As dean, I also launched a "Jesuit-in-Residence" initiative to provide co-curricular programming which challenges students to do good while doing well.

The city and its environs are home to Uber, Salesforce, WeWork, Twitter, and a host of other iconic companies. The city is also home to tens of thousands of homeless people, some of whom shoot drugs in plain sight. The response of some to this has been mostly dystopian. In one neighborhood residents got together and purchased truckloads of large boulders which they placed at strategic places in front of their multi-million dollar homes to prevent the homeless from camping out.

I am fortunate to work at a university, which values social and economic justice. I have also worked at schools, which did not think that these were important values. My challenge as Dean of the School of Management is figuring out ways to embed those values in all that we teach. It is entirely possible to start the next great company addressing all manner of consumer needs while ignoring the homeless veteran or single mom sitting in front of corporate headquarters with a needle in their veins.

I applaud the wonderful startups that are founded in San Francisco. I am certain that a scalable solution to the problem of the homeless can also be found here.

My doctoral research was an attempt to develop theories, which might impact the practices and policies associated with emergent communities. I now work in a prosperous community with a relatively progressive political ethos, but also one in which the economy is widely acknowledged to serve the interests of wealthy elites at the expense of the other classes. The research I did as an DM student certainly shaped by the readings, discussions (and arguments) over three years at Case Western Reserve University had a profound impact on me. In this sense, my work is incomplete.

Keywords
Networks, Community, Economic Empowerment, Entrepreneurship

About the Author: Charles T. Moses, DM
Dr. Moses is the Interim Dean of the School of Management at the University of San Francisco. He is the former Interim Dean of the Austin Peay State University College of Business Administration and Dean of the School of Business Administration at Clark Atlanta University, where he directed the University's Entrepreneurship and Innovation program. From 1994–2001, he was a consultant, based in South Africa and the Dean of Edupark, a business school affiliated with the University of in Polokwane, South Africa. Dr. Moses was also a Managing Director of Labat Africa, a consultancy and holding company there. His practice focused on acquisitions in Africa's fast-growing educational sector. During his tenure at Labat, he played a key role in the firm's listing on the "venture capital" board of the Johannesburg Stock Exchange. He is a 2004 graduate of the DM program.

Beth Fitz Gibbon

Without the research techniques I learned during the DM, including ethnography and interviewing, I would not have had the ability (or the guts) to take on an in-depth research process of that magnitude by myself. In addition, without the DM degree I would not have been entrusted with such an extensive and important undertaking.

Here Be Dragons

Following the dotcom boom and bust in 2001–2002, rising unemployment combined with downsizing, outsourcing, and outright firings from age discrimination led to a new boom: displaced workers marketing themselves as consultants. I had made my living as an independent consultant since 1994 while single-parenting two children. However, I could not afford to be labeled as a new market entrant. I needed to upgrade my value proposition and skills.

I am committed to lifelong learning. After getting my BA in the 1970's, I had taken executive education courses at Simmons Graduate School of Management in the 1980's. I earned my MBA and studied European Mergers and Acquisitions with PriceWaterhouse in Germany, Austria, and Hungary in the 1990's; and I attended a Wharton School executive education program in the early 2000's. However, I knew it was time to step up my game.

I had always dreamed of getting a PhD. The question was, in what area? I had been an undergraduate English major — a lover of books and writing. However, that was for personal pleasure, not professional credibility. Besides, how was I going to afford it, get through it while still working, and find a school that offered a program right for my life and my professional goals?

By 2005, my work was feeling redundant — different companies, same problems. So now, not only did I need a professional update, I was itch-ing for a big challenge. I was looking at university programs online, but none seemed right. I did not have time for a "real" (6–7 year) PhD. I did not want a deep dive into one subject (e.g., Accounting, Finance) and I did not plan to teach. As a self-directed, hands-on professional, I did not want to "administrate" either.

I had almost given up when an advertisement in *The Economist* caught my eye. It was for Case Western Reserve University's (CWRU) Doctor of Management (DM) Program. Now that was interesting. Who knew I could earn a DM degree?

I chose the Weatherhead program because CWRU is a world-class research institution and I wanted to earn the right to be a credible researcher. I wanted to have a respected voice based on my experience and the new research skills I could learn. Being a practitioner-scholar seemed the best way to leverage myself and my practice above the ordinary.

On the way home from interviews with the Director, John Aram, and a professor, Paul Salipante, I vacillated between thrilled and terrified. The DM program was exactly what I had been looking for; but was a rigorous 3-year commitment while working full-time the right thing to do? It turned out to be the best investment I have ever made.

The DM program was, for me, Joseph Campbell's classic hero journey. Like Odysseus, Frodo, and Harry Potter, I had a challenge, was often lost, and frequently afraid. I found my way along that road, because I had a brave cohort and all-knowing guides who appeared now and then to put me back on the trail when I would wander off to fight dragons. In addition, trust me, there were many to slay, the most fire-breathing one for me being statistics — which my study group referred to as "sadistics." *"Fantasy epics focus on a quest. The Ring must be destroyed, Voldemort must be defeated, Aslan must prevail. Pure-hearted underdogs triumph; kind and wise leaders restore order."* (New York Times, 2019). That was literally my epic journey throughout the DM program. My "kind and wise leader," Yoda, Gandalf, and Dumbledore all rolled into one, was my faculty advisor, Professor Bo Carlsson. Thanks to him, this "underdog" triumphed. Moreover, I could not be prouder of conquering statistics with the help of my study group and my quantitative advisor, Professor Toni Somers. Who would have guessed I would be able to question others' research based on my knowledge of SPSS and AMOS?

As an employee and consultant, I spent years working with global manufacturing companies in a variety of industries and capacities; from marketing and merchandising to R&D and new product development. I then went to strategic planning and on to entrepreneurial new venture development (i.e., joint ventures, strategic alliances, startups) However, R&D and manufacturing, the science and art of discovery and making things, were (and still are) my passions.

My research was about the consequences of outsourcing manufacturing, the separation of R&D from manufacturing, and implications for a company's future innovation capabilities. I wanted to figure out why my clients were giving away their brains (beyond the obvious bean counting) and what could be done to help them see things differently. I had no idea when I started down that dark road that I would emerge from my journey in a completely different space.

After graduation, I left the corporate for-profit world and landed in the nonprofit sector working for JumpStart, a funder of entrepreneurial high-tech startups with Intellectual Property (IP) and the likelihood of progressing through venture capital (VC) funding to acquisition, merger, or Initial Public Offering (IPO). Funded by the state of Ohio, they had been asked by the Economic Development Authority of the Federal Department of Commerce to help build similar entrepreneurial venture development organizations throughout the U.S. My new position as their first Chief Operating Officer was to build a national consulting arm for JumpStart and then act as Senior Advisor to client states and regions.

The CEO said he chose me because of my diverse industry experience, entrepreneurial consulting expertise, and a doctorate that would be respected by both the business world and the non-profit economic development world. I think the most valuable quality I contributed was the ability to span boundaries, a natural trait honed into a professional skill throughout the DM program. Thanks to wealthy foundation benefactors and deep government pockets, JumpStart had millions of dollars to bring into communities. What we did not have was an invitation.

The funders chose our clients. Sure, they wanted the money, but clients resented being told they would only get it if they let JumpStart guide their efforts. These were experienced economic development and business managers, angel and venture capital investors, university research commercialization experts, mayors, governors, and even McKinsey consultants who had been working with big cities.

Without the theoretical knowledge gained at Weatherhead, on topics as diverse as collective action, agency theory, organizational effectiveness, dynamic capabilities, and absorptive capacity, I would not have had the broad perspective required for approaching such diverse, public-private partnerships. I also would not have been able to manage the research processes required to delve deep into the economic and entrepreneurial ecosystems of diverse geographies such as Minneapolis Saint Paul, rural northern Indiana, and eastern upstate New York. In addition, without those experiences, I would never have seen my work presented to an international audience at The Brookings Institution in Washington D.C.

Shortly after relocating to Portland, Oregon a few years later, I received a call from a DM classmate who was giving me a heads-up that some economic development people from Portland would contact me. He had met them when they came to northeast Ohio to learn how the region was supporting manufacturing. Classmates from the DM program continue to be friends and valuable networking assets.

> **My DM degree is the best investment I ever made because not only has it earned me career longevity, it has given me the ability to contribute on a much broader scale and scope than I ever thought possible.**

That introduction led to my being retained by the Portland, Oregon/ Vancouver, Washington region to develop research for a grant funded by U.S. Departments of Commerce, Defense, Labor, and Energy, the Small Business Administration, and the National Institute of Standards & Technology. Over two years my research produced four extensive, complex reports with recommendations for expanding the states' economies through advanced manufacturing and exports:

1. Making Prosperity: Creating a Sound Economy through Advanced Manufacturing, Advanced Materials and Robust Supply Chains
2. Powering the Future of Manufacturing with Computers & Electronics
3. Additive & Subtractive: The New Math of Metals & Machinery
4. Flying into the Future with Aerospace & Defense

Without the research techniques I learned during the DM, including ethnography and interviewing, I would not have had the ability (or the guts) to take on an in-depth research process of that magnitude by myself. In addition, without the DM degree I would not have been entrusted with such an extensive and important undertaking.

Researching and writing those reports gave me the background and forward-looking knowledge of manufacturing possessed by few others in Oregon. Therefore, the State then retained me to research and write the Oregon Talent Plan and to help startup the Oregon Talent Council based on my research findings. Its objectives were:

1. Support Oregon manufacturing businesses with a pipeline of educated, trained, work-ready, technology-based incumbent, and potential employees
2. Develop working alliances among tech schools, community colleges, universities, economic development agencies, and public & private companies in support of industrial workforce needs

The abilities I gained through the DM program enabled me to dig deeper with statistical research, to integrate divergent perspectives, and to have an authoritative voice for both industry and economic development.

When I completed that assignment, the State of Oregon and the Oregon Institute of Technology retained me to help startup the Oregon Manufacturing Innovation Center — OMIC R&D: A Research and Development partnership focused on metals and new materials for advanced manufacturing. Sponsored by Boeing, Daimler, Mitsubishi, and other world-leading corporations, members include smaller businesses, universities, and economic development agencies. The research I had completed, plus my business background in manufacturing and R&D, and my experience with startups and partnership alliances, enabled me to work with the Board of Governors to build OMIC's five-year strategic plan and governance structure. I developed the nonprofit by-laws, helped design the organizational structure, created the website content, and helped build the first year quarterly operational plan. Then I worked with university and industry engineering and metallurgy members to develop OMIC R&D's Research Roadmap.

Conclusion

Without completing the DM, I would never have had the research capability or the professional credibility to deliver all those measurable outcomes and returns on investment for state and regional clients as well as businesses. Yes, the DM degree opened doors for me. More importantly, the DM education allowed me to expand my practice beyond working with manufacturing companies to working on behalf of manufacturers. I still consult with companies that want to grow or diversify, but now I also get to advocate for them on the public and nonprofit sides.

The DM Program fulfilled my initial goals: get a degree, learn to do good research, and differentiate myself as a consultant. It also exceeded my expectations. The thought-provoking, mind-expanding class discussions about ethics and global political and economic challenges with business and nonprofit leaders from around the world was an extraordinary experience I miss to this day. This is why I look forward to DM/PhD reunions every two years. My cohort included people from Egypt, Africa, and Myanmar, the U.S. west coast, east coast, and in-between. That diversity enriched us all.

My DM degree is the best investment I ever made because not only has it earned me career longevity, it has given me the ability to contribute on a much broader scale and scope than I ever thought possible.

Because of my commitment to the program, I was a proud member of the Weatherhead DM/PhD. Advisory Council from 2009 through 2013. In 2018, I was honored to accept the role of Chairperson of the Council. The DM program's rigor, a minimum of 20–30 hours per week of schoolwork on top of a heavy practitioner workload, refined my planning, prioritizing, and time management skills. It also reinforced the need to engage with and depend on a trusted team, because you will never conquer all the dragons without them. That experience has enabled me to work full time, manage council responsibilities, and still have a "real life." In addition, I am now a Research Fellow at Weatherhead, pursuing new interests arising from my expanded career on the public-private partnership side of manufacturing. My practitioner-scholar journey is taking me again on the road to new discoveries.

Keywords

Consulting, Practitioner-Scholar, Advanced Manufacturing, DM Advisory Council

About the Author: Beth Fitz Gibbon, DM

Dr. Fitz Gibbon is founder and president of Pathfox Venture Development, designing new business initiatives to help manufacturing companies grow. She also collaborates with national and statewide entities to plan and execute strategies for enhancing supply chains, entrepreneurial ecosystems, and inclusive talent pools. She has extensive experience with public/private partnerships and strategic alliances in both the industrial and public sectors. Dr. Fitz Gibbon earned her Doctor of Management at Case Western Reserve University, an MBA in International Business at Emory, and a BA at Rutgers.

Bernard C. Bailey

What I never anticipated when beginning the journey from CEO to practitioner-scholar was how it would transform my thinking and approach to both problem solving and management — well beyond my doctoral studies in boardroom decision making.

The Journey from CEO to Practitioner Scholar

Introduction and Problem of Practice

At no time since the Great Depression and the subsequent establishment of the Security and Exchange Commission (SEC) has the United States gone through a greater shake-up of corporate governance than the decade of the 2000s. The accounting scandal and fraud that led to the collapse and dissolution of Enron — what had been the seventh largest company by total sales in America — serves as the poster child for dysfunctional corporate governance. Early in the decade, a less talked about governance crisis resulted in the destruction of more than $1.5 trillion in shareholder value: the technology bubble. This collapse was driven by ill-conceived strategies that were poorly, and in some cases fraudulently, executed by management, all under the watchful (or closed) eyes of incompetent boards of directors. The Global Financial Crisis of 2008, far larger and significantly more complex than the technology bubble's collapse, rocked the foundations of the global financial system. While not directly attributable to a systemic governance failure, the failure of individual boards within the financial sector to adequately understand and monitor the risk profiles and the excessive risk taking promoted by financial executive incentive systems certainly contributed to the failure.

The response to governance failures during this decade was the passage of two sweeping legislative bills, which served to dramatically alter the governance landscape across America. Additionally, the major stock exchanges mandated a series of actions that served to enhance the power of boards of directors relative to management through greater independence and accountability.

It is within this environment that as a CEO responsible for the management of a publicly traded company, as well as a director and board chairman for four additional publicly traded firms that I began to question the effectiveness of these policies to address the waning trust in corporate America. More importantly, it called to question the entire system of capitalism that had so effectively empowered citizens throughout the globe to realize unprecedented advances in their standards of living. This led me on a four-year inquiry and discovery process through the Doctor of Management (DM) programs, a practitioner scholar program, at Case Western Reserve University (CWRU). This journey was one filled by my awakening to a body of knowledge and an ontological experience that was well beyond any expectation I could have reasonably imagined when I began the process.

Research and Findings

The study of corporate governance is one of the most studied areas in business research. Unfortunately, the vast body of research has been focused on confounding empirical evidence that has failed to provide little understanding regarding the behavioral processes and dynamics associated with board decision making despite the fact that the potent reminder from the Enron disaster is "good governance comes down to directors making good decisions" (Useem, 2003, p. 247). Leveraging my network and relationships amongst the corporate director community, I was able to undertake a comprehensive mixed methods study, including sequential qualitative and quantitative analyses, of board decision-making processes. The conclusions from this research resulted in a deeper understanding of how directors, acting as a consensus decision-making body, make more effective decisions that result in better outcomes that in turn result in a reinforcing process of enhanced respect and trust amongst the board members and between the board members and the executive management teams over whom they are responsible for exercising oversight.

This research has served to inform additional board scholarship, having been cited in more than 40 articles in the past six years. In addition to publishing this work in a peer-reviewed journal on corporate governance,

I have presented this work in multiple conferences on corporate governance and served as an expert witness in the Delaware Court of Chancery, the nation's most distinguished court on corporate governance.

Personal Transformation

What I never anticipated when beginning the journey from CEO to practitioner-scholar was how it would transform my thinking and approach to both problem solving and management — well beyond my doctoral studies in boardroom decision making. After graduation, I returned to the commercial sector in the position of Chairman and CEO of a private equity backed global company. I also continued to serve on multiple publicly traded company boards, eventually serving as chairman of the board for two of these companies. Embodying the principles of procedural justice, trust, and effective decision making — all theoretical constructs examined and developed during my research process — allowed me to evolve my own managerial style to one of greater collaboration, empathy, and inquiry. Data analysis and evidence-based inquiries coupled with more robust discussions and theoretically grounded processes became more the norm as we looked to evolve our strategic direction. With an insatiable curiosity that led me to search for both relevant and appropriate methods and tools for our company's transformation, I, paradoxically, as a result of my grounding in theory and scholarship became a much more discerning consumer of management theory (Christensen & Raynor, 2003). While previously every new management practice, complete with impressive stories about how companies had successfully applied these practices to achieve remarkable success, appeared to be a shiny objective worthy of pursuit, now I was able to apply a more rigorous approach to understand what constituted sound management theory and practices for our unique situation. More importantly, these principles of inquiry, analysis, and contextualism I learned during my doctoral studies were permeated through the organization.

After six years serving as Chairman and CEO, our company was sold allowing me a period of introspection to discern my next career move. While continuing to serve on several boards of directors, both for-profit and not-for-profit, I have transitioned my experience as a CEO and practitioner scholar to address economic issues in the public policy arena. Today, I serve as the President of the Committee for Economic Development (CED) of The Conference Board, a Washington, DC based nonpartisan think tank addressing economic issues in our nation's interests. The ability to both write and evaluate rigorous scholarly research, combined with my practical knowledge as a CEO in understanding how public policy decisions effect practitioners who have to live with the consequences of these decisions, has allowed me to further extend my career into the arena of public policy think tanks.

Reflections

My journey into the academy started as a simple inquiry to understand how boards of directors might serve more effectively in protecting the interests of shareholders and greater society. Through the process of inquiry and discovery, I was introduced to a world of scholarship and intellect that I had never experienced in my previous undergraduate and graduate studies. Concepts, theories and research in the areas of psychology, sociology, economics, governance, management, law, public policy, ethics, and philosophy were opened to me as part of my own self-discovery process. The application of this scholarship has made me a better board member, executive and citizen. More importantly, it has served to embolden me to challenge, as well as explore, new arenas of inquiry, insight and action.

Keywords

Governance, Inquiry, Practitioner, Theory, Shareholders

About the Author: Bernard C. Bailey, PhD

Dr. Bailey serves as the President of the Committee for Economic Development. He also serves on the boards of directors of three private equity backed companies, a publicly traded company, as well as two not-for-profit boards, including Chairman of Trout Unlimited, a 160,000-member cold-water conservation organization. Previously, he served as CEO of three companies, two public, and one private. Dr. Bailey has also served as director of eight publicly traded companies.

Sherry Sanger

The most unexpected and memorable part of the program was the opportunity to be part of a scholarly community and build lifelong friendships, collaborations, and partnerships. I came for a degree and discovered an unexpected benefit by encountering people like myself who are consummate explorers and learners. People who love to talk about ideas, are interested in different perspectives, and want to impact the world.

Exploring. Connecting. Impacting.

I love to explore. Always have. And, so far, it's led to some pretty interesting discoveries and experiences. The itch to explore probably originates from a childhood spent on the move. We moved every few years growing up, which made our physical homes less important than the people in them. I added a couple more geographic milestones to my path during my undergraduate years that included adventures in Europe for both work and study. I discovered a love for learning new things that took me well beyond the coursework required for my German literature major. I pursued elective coursework to attain a private pilot's license and built my skills in darkroom photography. As I bridged into the business world following an MBA and spent time in finance, new product development, and marketing, I found that each of those disparate experiences from my past prepared and primed me to think creatively, strategically and analytically in each of the roles I progressed through. However, as I sat in my office 10 years ago, I wanted to make sure that I would continue to be able to do so.

Why a Doctorate?
In 2010, I was working as the Vice President of Marketing in an incredible firm with leaders I respected greatly, but felt the urge to explore, learn, and continue to grow. However, I did not want to change companies to do so, as seemed to be the common path for many marketing leaders. I enjoyed the people I was working with and my growing responsibilities. At the time, our firm continued to enjoy incredible growth and seemed well poised for the future, but we did not want to

take our success for granted. The world around us was changing rapidly. Digital and mobile technologies along with data and analytics were changing the business landscape. Iconic firms were starting to stumble. Firms like Blockbuster and Kodak, darlings of their industries, were facing unexpected and unprecedented challenges from emerging competitors that, with the benefit of hindsight, we now know changed their industries forever. So, I decided to explore a path to learning and development that would benefit me and the organization I worked for. I decided to pursue a residency-based PhD program that provided an in-class experience while remaining in practice. Finally, I embarked on a research agenda that focused on understanding how leaders stay open to new ideas.

Connecting & Exploring in the Doctor of Management (DM) Program
As I reflect on my experiences in the program and with my research, I see two primary benefits. First, the program wired me for connections. The most unexpected and memorable part of the program was the opportunity to be part of a scholarly community and build lifelong friendships, collaborations, and partnerships. I came for a degree and discovered an unexpected benefit by encountering people like myself who are consummate explorers and learners. People who love to talk about ideas, are interested in different perspectives, and want to impact the world.

Second, the program allowed me to explore my own boundaries. The interdisciplinary nature of the program allowed me to take coursework across a variety of domains to broaden my thinking, courses like collective action, systems thinking, and design & innovation. This challenged me to think about the world beyond the walls of the organization. The exposure to multiple research methods took my research and analytical skills to a new level of rigor. The opportunity to do qualitative interviews, a quantitative survey, and an experiment allowed me to explore diverse avenues to answering my research questions. This exploration around new ideas and new research techniques helped me enhance my critical and analytical thinking in ways that have benefited me and my organization significantly since finishing the program.

Post Program Impact
Throughout the program, I learned about myself. I renewed my love for learning, teaching, and research, but I also realized that I still love

impacting the world of practice. And, most importantly, I decided that I wanted to continue to have a foot in both worlds – the academy and practice, which I have done. Straddling these two worlds has been incredibly impactful, as my experiences in practice and in academia continue to build on each other in impactful ways. Let me share a few examples.

Career Growth

The PhD experience enhanced my thinking in a way that allowed me to elevate my contributions in my organization. I began to think about my leadership, our organizational challenges, and market opportunities more expansively, strategically, and critically. This has led to additional responsibilities and career growth during and after the program. Today, in addition to Marketing, I lead our digital customer experience, market intelligence, and new product development efforts related to emerging technology and potential sources of disruption.

Data & Analytics Leadership

Upskilling my analytical toolkit could not have been timelier. Upon entering the program, I had been doing market research for a long time. I anticipated that growing my research skills would allow me to lead a higher performing research function. What I did not fully anticipate is the pace at which the need for data and analytics would accelerate in our organization and function. While I was in the program, the revolution of data and analytics was quickly unfolding. The PhD poised me to lead our efforts related to advanced customer data and connected analytics, which we see as critical to our competitive differentiation strategy both today and in the future.

Applying Research in Practice

Today's business environment is marked by a clear sense of change, growth, and volatility. Imagining future possibilities is becoming an increasingly critical capacity among leaders that is not confined to any particular management discipline. While the popular literature is full of tips, tricks, models, techniques, and tools, these various strategy tools and frameworks seem to be failing leaders. Spotting changing market dynamics and discerning opportunities rely on a leader's ability to connect the dots — what they see as critical vs. inconsequential, what they assess as opportunities vs. threats, and ultimately what they decide to invest time, money, and effort in. I became passionate about providing new insight into how leaders can stay open to new information and ideas. How do they prevent becoming entrenched in their thinking as they move through their career? In the program, my co-authors and I received three best paper awards at academic conferences for our work that uncovered and tested deliberate strategies that leaders employ to disrupt their own thinking and circumvent entrenchment. After the program, I applied my research in practice to inspire a culture of openness and curiosity. I have presented my research at practitioner conferences and have utilized several strategies based on my research findings for myself and in my organization.

Our organization just celebrated 50 years in business, and we are blessed by incredible loyalty, tenure, and growth. With tenure comes deep experience and knowledge, but it also means that we need to constantly challenge ourselves to avoid entrenchment. My research was inspired by this challenge. How can successful organizations like ours with experienced leaders that have been able to see around corners, continue to do so? What I found is that when primed, leaders generate ideas that are less incremental and internally focused. This finding led to the introduction of a new market intelligence process and series of discussions focused on exploration and discovery, designed to challenge our thinking and bring the outside in. We took some of the trends that were emerging in our industry like shared, autonomous, electric and connected and looked at them from all angles. We talked to all the players — the academics, the consultants, the start-ups, and the legacy organizations — to understand the technology involved, the forces driving the trends, the challenges, the forecasts. Building on my research, we intentionally sought out opposing views. And then formed our own perspective and looked at the opportunities to position the organization for the best possible future. This work has certainly enhanced our leader's peripheral vision, but it has also led to distinct investment, new product development and incubation strategies that have helped us differentiate ourselves in the marketplace.

> This exploration around new ideas and new research techniques helped me enhance my critical and analytical thinking in ways that have benefited me and my organization significantly since finishing the program.

Inspiring Broader Thinking

Again, building on my research I developed strategies to expose my leadership to new ideas and experiences that are outside the industry. The goal was to prevent entrenched thinking in the team and cultivate broad thinking. To accomplish this, I sponsored a series of learning events with my leadership team, designed specifically to broaden and extend their thinking. We went to a different city for each of the four events, which were spaced several months apart. In each city, the team was exposed to a variety of stimuli and experiences — historical sites, maker spaces, start-ups, exhibits, performances — and a variety of people — artists, chefs, entrepreneurs, craftsmen, and musicians. Each team member was given a journal to capture their reflections, what they noticed and saw that impacted them from these multi-disciplinary experiences. And then we talked about those learnings. About what they liked, what made them uncomfortable, what they got excited about, and how it relates back to our work as marketers, designers, and technologists? The results have been profound in terms of inspiring creative thinking, building a shared culture of learning and bringing the outside in, fostering a sense of team and leading culture and innovation in our organization.

Teacher & Coach

I have also had the opportunity to work, teach, and coach in the DM program and have thoroughly enjoyed the opportunity to encourage early scholars as they begin their research journey. In turn, teaching and coaching inspires me to continue my own research.

On Straddling Academia & Practice

Some of the toughest challenges that need to be tackled in business will be best tackled by drawing on talent from both sides — academia and practice. This will be an important bridge for many of us to straddle in the future. I look forward to being a part of building that bridge.

Keywords
Marketing, Disruption, Exploring, Connecting, and Impacting

About the Author: Sherry Sanger, PhD
Dr. Sanger is Executive Vice President of Marketing for Penske Transportation Solutions, an $8.4 billion leader in transportation and logistics that operates a fleet of more than 300,000 vehicles with a global workforce of more than 36,000 people. Dr. Sanger holds a bachelor's degree in German from Kent State University, a master's degree in international management from the Thunderbird School of Global Management, an MBA from Case Western Reserve University, and a PhD in management from Case Western Reserve University. She lives with her husband Tim and they have two children, Lindsay and Caden.

*"In learning you will teach,
in teaching you will learn."*

Phil Collins

Educator

Developing the ability to
shape the environment from
DM programmatic ideals
and curriculum

Antoinette La Belle

The program would, for me, be a means to "refresh and reset". While I originally thought I would return to continue my private sector career, in reality the program provided me the space to more seriously contemplate my future and my next professional chapter.

A Narrative: Transformative Journey of a Nonprofit Leader and Practitioner Scholar

This narrative reflects two paths that emerged because of my doctoral research: path one was my contribution — based on original research — to the field of leadership development in the nonprofit sector; the second path is more personal and reflects what I personally and professionally derived from my leader/learner journey in the doctorate program.

For my practitioner scholar colleagues, I share what was my small contribution to the very large field of leadership development, including its focus in the nonprofit sector, a less crowded field in terms of available research and extant resources. Some of the described results are, in part, a "connecting of the dots" based on my background as an organization and talent development practitioner and my professional connections in the field.

My research was born out of what I came to realize was a fierce debate based on a perception that the better organizational leaders came from the private sector, not the nonprofit sector. Having worked in the private sector for my career but having the benefit of rewarding nonprofit board service, as well as knowing several exceptional nonprofit leaders, my research was focused on ending this debate by either validating or dispelling this perception. Without going into a detailed construction of my research methodology, the net result of my research may be distilled into one salient, fact based, data driven finding: sector origin (e.g., private, public, or nonprofit) of a leader bears no relevance (i.e., causation or correlation) to leadership effectiveness. Rather, the *diversity* of professional experience (i.e., the complexity of a leader's *behavioral repertoire*) is the differentiator in being more or less effective as a leader.

A brief overview of behavioral repertoire as it relates to leaders may be useful context. To summarize, drawing on the work of Lawrence, Lenk & Quinn, 2009 but without any of the many nuances, behavioral repertoire refers to the skills derived from different experiences that accrete to a professional and are evidenced across four "competing values" for effectiveness: collaborate, create, compete, and control. Leaders with higher assessments in these areas (either by self or by others) are deemed to have a more *complex* behavioral repertoire. They are better equipped and more skilled — often with incomplete information or deep subject matter expertise — to assess and adapt to new and/or complex work situations by relying on their knowledge drawn from diverse prior experiences they have navigated. In my research, multi-sector experience, or having worked in *all* three sectors, was the proxy for diversity of experience; leaders with multi-sector experience scored higher than others in my research survey.

In retrospect after completing my doctorate, I consider this an *outward facing* assessment perspective. I did not focus on another potential benefit from those who took the survey. The Bridgespan Group for their Leaders Matter publication also interviewed two nonprofit leaders I know who took my survey in 2010. One had a revelation that she was actually more competitive than she thought (and for a good outcome in competing for funding). The other made sure to staff for strength (i.e., hire someone who could augment his strengths by bringing strength to areas that were not his). These I consider powerful, instructive, *inward facing* self-assessments.

Both outward and inward facing perspectives are important "tent poles" for leadership development: having strong pattern identification, sense making, problem solving, and adaptive capacity skills in leading an organization. Further, having the power of self-reflection and self-knowledge, knowing one's strengths as well as potential development pitfalls, in leading an organization is also important. Both perspectives fueled and bolstered some of my subsequent organization and talent development work and research dissemination strategies. I use the framing concept of behavioral repertoire when assessing talent and succession planning. I now have a finer grained means for unpacking a resume and making some initial assessments about potential candidates based on the diversity of their career trajectory. In my first role after the program where I was the East Coast Director for the Encore Fellowship Program, an initiative of Encore.org, I was responsible for assessing mid-career candidates from the for profit sector who wanted to actually move into roles in the nonprofit sector. While I knew nonprofit leaders would value the technical skills of fellows, the more critical assessment I made was judgments about a candidate's "behavioral repertoire" and their adaptive capacity — and humility — to successfully move into the sector. Ultimately, about two in five applicants advanced to being considered for these highly valued fellowships.

In subsequent roles, I continue to use the behavioral repertoire framework in sourcing and recruiting candidates and in coaching professionals about their career development. As I have moved into progressively more responsible nonprofit leadership roles at other organizations, I use the behavioral repertoire framework for my own self-assessment of how I am dealing with the competing role demands as a nonprofit leader. I am often confronted with decisions that need to be made which are significantly more complex — in resourced constrained environments — where all strategic choices (e.g., seeking alliances/partnership, making strategic pivots based on funding) have some organizational tradeoffs.

A more important result also occurred from my research work with my nonprofit colleagues. They were heartened by my findings since they frequently heard in their careers that nonprofit work was "easier" or required less skill, which for anyone working in the sector knows is emphatically *not* the case. That said, while the behavioral repertoire framework and competing role demands provided means to think about their career growth, they also felt they had fewer ways — including financial resources — or avenues for important professional development experiences. As I contemplated this challenge, I recall learning from Dr. Paul Salipante, Professor Emeritus and one of my research advisors, the theory of *situated learning* and Lave & Wenger's work in this area. While more involved than my summary here, learning is contextual within the environment and/or culture of an experience. From my organization development work in the private sector, this theory runs parallel to work done in the area of the "lessons of experience" from the Center for Creative Leadership (CCL); how to think about, mine insights, and learn from work experiences. It is the sentiment from my nonprofit colleagues and my understanding about situated learning and the lessons of experience that ultimately was the basis for an important collaboration that I conceived of and facilitated. The collaboration ultimately resulted in one means to address this development "opportunity deficit" for nonprofit professionals. With the benefit of hindsight, the collaboration and outcome could be thought of as *"paying it forward."*

I reached out to Cindy McCauley, Senior Fellow at the Center for Creative Leadership, who has a specialty of experience-driven leadership development and whose work I had used in the past. I approached her about experience-driven research for nonprofit leaders and learned that, at the time that was not a focus for CCL. While it was a much longer journey than anticipated from an initial idea to reality, the result of that discussion with Cindy led to a collaboration between CCL and professional friends at Community Resource Exchange (CRENYC), which ultimately resulted in *Meeting the Job Challenges of Nonprofit Leaders — A field book on Strategies and Action* by Jean Lobell, Mohan Sikka, and Pavitra Menon — a learning from doing guide of suggested development approaches. I recently reached out to CRENYC to find out how the work has progressed since their guide was published. According to Jean Lobell, the book "spawned interest in several fronts" and "the framework that served as the core of the guide's content was used in our leadership development programs." Further, the *Nonprofit Quarterly* asked CRE to write an article about self-coaching (one recommended strategy in the field book); that article was voted as one of the "top 40 NPQ articles in 2017". As a side note, originally CCL, CRE, and I had hoped I would be part of the field book writing team. However, my own professional transition and crossover to the nonprofit sector from the private sector required my dedicated focus and energy.

In the category that timing can sometimes be everything, The Bridgespan Group, previously mentioned, and Board Source — both well-known and regarded advisory organizations to the nonprofit sector and where I had professional connections — supported disseminating my research due to the topical relevance of a way to confront the challenge of a projected nonprofit leadership shortage. My research work and subsequent articles aligned with the mission of each organization — strengthening nonprofits as they address society's challenges. There was also an added value proposition for all parties — they gained access to disseminating original research on a critical, timely leadership topic; I gained the value of having my research disseminated by widely recognized organizations, each having wide distribution networks. It was also a period when the economy was in serious recession and many private sector professionals for whom their roles no longer existed were contemplating "crossing over" to roles in the nonprofit sector. Regardless of the possible boost of these circumstances in creating greater interest in my research, I remain gratified of hitting on an important research topic that contributed to the field and to its reception in the nonprofit sector. Subsequent to these pathways, however, there

> My path has been significantly altered by my participation in and the opportunities provided to me in the program.

has been little follow-on activity or inbound inquiry about my research. While the topic is essentially timeless, I have learned over my own nonprofit career that these types of organizations are constantly seeking out and publishing new content to their stakeholders to stay relevant; as such, I have learned that topical relevance can be short lived. That aside, I have an invitation from Bridgespan should I wish to write a follow-up article.

Now, to the second path, which is more personal in nature. In reflecting on creating this narrative, I reread my original application submission from January 2007, more than 12 years ago. Despite the unanticipated research topic and its practical applications, the theme that emerged from my application was of being on a learning journey, which the doctoral program would provide — and not of professional advancement or achievement. I quoted John Gardener ("Don't set out in life to be an interesting person; set out to be an interested person" — Goldsmith et al., 2000, p. 14) and Jim Collins (be "someone who learns not because it will get them somewhere but, rather, to see learning as part of the reason for living and where there is no economic justification for learning — performance is not the ultimate "why" of learning — learning is the "why" — Goldsmith et al., 2000, p. 14). At the time of application, I had already worked for more than 35 years in the private sector. While I was not "done" with a professional career, I felt stale and my learning stance had narrowed. The program would, for me, be a means to "refresh and reset". While I originally thought I would return to continue my private sector career, in reality the program provided me the space to more seriously contemplate my future and my next professional chapter. Ultimately, it became an unintended but personal and professional pivot for me.

In taking stock after graduation, I realized that, if possible, I wanted to actually continue the next phase of my career in the nonprofit sector. I had learned a great deal about the sector and had met a wide range of exceptional nonprofit professionals and leaders who had been very generous in sharing their own stories and insights with me in the course of my research. I felt the time might be right to leverage all that I learned. While no doubt my doctoral research contributed to the desire to shift my professional energies, I would be remiss if I did not share that the ongoing and deepening economic recession and financial crisis, among other factors, contributed to my mindset shift from commercially focused to mission focused work. That aside, doing social good has been an important value imbued to me from an early age; my nonprofit board service was one important expression of that value, especially in my private sector career. Actively attempting to move into the nonprofit sector could be a career capstone and professional legacy if I could align my professional career with doing greater social purpose work.

I am now in my ninth year and my third nonprofit leadership role. I truly am "living my research" and frequently think — "ah, so that is what they meant" when I recall some of the struggles described in my qualitative interviews with executives who, like me, crossed over from the private into the nonprofit sector. For example, I now understand and deal with the more diffuse power structures and multiple, external stakeholders such as funders who can — at times — influence strategic work which subsequently requires special effort to ensure that a clear line of sight with our mission holds true; the difference between placed-based work in a national nonprofit structure and the challenge of giving voice to relevant local differences that should be factored into the strategy; where the strength of the relationship between the board chair and nonprofit leader can either lift the strategic vision about the work or drive decisions with incomplete or inaccurate information and require spending the resources of time and expertise to explain why a course of action may be flawed; or how isolating the role can be as a nonprofit leader. To this specific point, my research found that leaders who come from within the sector usually have an already built in network of nonprofit professionals for advice, a kitchen cabinet, so to speak; my professional network remains largely based on relationships built from my own nonprofit board work and my private sector career. I suspect I still may miss some of the mission driven, deeper insights and approaches due to my more corporate mindset, although hopefully my mindset is more hybrid by now. Fortunately, I also use the advice I heard from one of my qualitative research interviews — to find the "wise souls" that may exist in an organization; these are the individuals who provide me with unfiltered views and advice about my ideas and perspectives. These challenges reflect some of my own lessons from experience and situated learning…girded by an understructure from my research. They are, however, far outweighed with the rewards of doing social purpose and systems change work.

I am doing work that I did not envision 12 years ago when I entered the doctorate program. My path has been significantly altered by my participation in and the opportunities provided to me in the program. I am gratified on at least two fronts: that I had a research topic that was valued in the field and of interest to others; and that I was guided by and benefited from the wisdom and engagement of my professors, advisors and nonprofit leaders who willingly shared their own stories. I hope to remain on a continuous voyage of discovery and learning journey in my career and life.

Keywords

Behavioral Repertoire, Competing Values Framework, Crossover Nonprofit Leaders

About the Author: Antoinette (Toni) La Belle, DM

Dr. La Belle, DM, is currently Senior Advisor with JUST Capital, having retired as Chief Operating Officer and Managing Director, Justness for JUST Capital at the end of 2019. She continues to advise and provide thought leadership on Human Capital Management internally for the organization and on various Human Capital research components that are a part of the JUST overall rankings and company evaluation process. She also supports the organization externally to advance its mission and work.

Dr. La Belle spent most of her career in the private sector as an executive working in the areas of organization development, strategic business and human capital strategies, and change management initiatives. She concluded her corporate career in 2007 as a Managing Director at Lehman Brothers to enter a doctoral program at Case Western Reserve University, Weatherhead School of Management and to continue her civic engagement endeavors. Her doctoral research was a comparison study of the professional and situational influences on nonprofit leaders' effectiveness; The Bridgespan Group and Board Source have featured articles based on her research.

Dr. La Belle's numerous civic engagement activities focus on initiatives and organizations that help "level the playing field" by working for social and economic justice and well-being for all. In addition to her doctorate, Dr. La Belle holds an MBA from Fordham University and a BS from Marymount College and is an arbitrator with FINRA (Financial Industry Regulatory Authority).

Stephen P. Miller

In my case the program helped me achieve a life-long personal goal and become a more effective teacher and consultant and now it informs my teaching and consulting practice in ways that previously could not have been imagined.

Building and Sustaining a Family Business

Earning a PhD from the Doctor of Management (DM) Program at Case Western Reserve University (CWRU) was one of the most meaningful experiences of my life, from both personal and professional development perspectives.

From a personal perspective, it allowed me to "scratch an itch" that I had felt for 30 years to earn a terminal degree. From a professional perspective, it allowed me to build on over three decades of experience as a family business leader to more deeply explore and understand factors that contribute to the development of leadership talent among next-generation family members in family-owned enterprises.

In this essay, I will address how the DM program satisfied that personal "itch," summarize the implications of my research for practice, and provide examples of how the research has helped me be a more effective in my roles as professor of the practice of family business at the University of North Carolina's Kenan-Flagler Business School and consultant to a number of large family firms.

Scratching the Itch

In my first residency, Dr. Richard Boyatzis, who later became my subject area advisor and dissertation committee chair, asked us what mid-life crisis we were trying to address through participation in the DM program. He went on to explain that research suggests that there really is something to the "seven-year itch." Research shows that humans experience psychological and physiological changes about every seven years or so, and that those changes are often accompanied by an examination of how our lives are progressing. I quickly did the math as I was age 56. Let's see, 7 x 8 = 56. That really hit home with me. While I did not feel I was in crisis mode, I did know at a very deep level that something was missing in my life.

Upon reflection, I remembered that my career goal when I first finished college was to work for a couple of years — I needed the money — then go back to law school. Through incredibly good fortune, my first job out of school turned into a 34-year career working as a senior non-family executive in a family owned firm that was growing rapidly. I found myself on the ground floor of a great opportunity working for a family for whom I had deep respect in my hometown — one with a mission that extended beyond just making money. It was a career that allowed me to learn and express creativity, entrepreneurship, and leadership skills, including the freedom to make mistakes. Shortly after beginning that career, I was blessed with a wonderful wife and two magnificent daughters, so I never looked back.

> **The CWRU program is designed to teach the research skills needed to "bridge the gap" between academics and practitioners.**

Still, there was this lingering feeling that I had never really "finished" my formal education. I am curious by nature and really love school and the process of learning new things. I had returned to my alma mater, The University of North Carolina (UNC) Chapel Hill, for a year-long executive program and to a similar program at Harvard a number of years later to keep my business education current. Those were transformative experiences, but they were not degree programs, so I still felt like there was something missing in my education.

Several years before entering CWRU's DM Program, I began teaching a class on family business at UNC's Kenan-Flagler Business School as an adjunct professor. How that came about is another story, but my primary motivation was to "give back" to the state-supported university that had made it possible for me to acquire my college degree. As a practitioner, I had become a student of family business, which began to emerge as an academic discipline during the early years of my career. I had studied pretty much everything I could get my hands on as I found it immediately applicable to my role as a leader in a third-generation family firm whose owners wanted it to continue as an evergreen family-owned enterprise. I had also become personally acquainted with a number of the early academic pioneers in the field, several of whom helped me design my family business class at UNC.

What I learned was that there was a need for more empirical research in many areas of family business, including the one that was nearest and dearest to my heart — leadership development among next-generation family firm leaders. I had fallen in love with my students and wanted to do everything I could to help them decide if working in their family firms was the best life decision for them and, if it was, what they could do to prepare for the complex challenges of leading a family enterprise. And there was still this "itch," which only became stronger the more I was around academics who knew how to do world-class research.

I seemed too old to pursue a PhD, and I was certainly too old to pursue a tenure track professorship, which was not really my goal. I just wanted to learn how to do research in the area that interested me and to finally "scratch that itch" of completing a terminal degree. So, what to do? I really had no idea.

I was fortunate that two of my professor friends at UNC knew about the DM program at CWRU and suggested that I explore that as a possibility. There must have been divine intervention as when I called and talked to Sue Nartker and Dr. Kalle Lyytinen to learn about the program, they were preparing for the inaugural International Conference on Engaged Management Scholarship and invited me to attend. Academics and practitioners enrolled in engaged scholarship programs around the world assembled at CWRU to share experiences and research. I quickly learned that CWRU pioneered the idea of providing rigorous training for mid-career practitioners who were interested in learning how to do research and wanted to earn a degree beyond a master's degree. I also learned that I could quickly identify CWRU DM students from the high quality of their presentations at the conference.

Following the conference, Sue suggested that I speak with Dr. Richard Boyatzis as he shared my interest in family enterprises. I was familiar with Richard's work on leadership and emotional social intelligence and wondered if such an accomplished academic would really be interested in what I wanted to do. To my surprise and delight, Richard spent an hour on the phone with me, understood exactly what I wanted to accomplish, demonstrated his own enthusiasm for family business, and offered to be my subject area advisor if I enrolled in the program. I had found my place.

Four years later, I walked across the stage at Severance Hall, received my PhD. diploma, and was hooded by Richard. The itch was scratched. I will be forever grateful to Richard, my subject area advisor and dissertation committee chair, Kalle, my methods advisor and member of my dissertation committee, Sue, Marilyn, and all the professors who taught in the DM Program during my years at CWRU.

Summary of Research Implications for Practice
Building and sustaining a family business is hard work. Thirty percent of family businesses survive from the first to the second generation of family ownership, only 12% survive from the second generation to the third, and only 4% survive from the third generation to the fourth. One of the leading causes of family business failure is weak next-generation leadership. Overcoming the obstacles of successfully founding a business, keeping up with changes in the marketplace, taking care of employees and customers, raising capital, and developing tax-efficient ownership structures require careful planning, skillful execution, and a lot of energy. As important as those tasks are, when it comes to preparing next-generation family members for leadership and ownership responsibilities, my study provided empirical evidence that what happens in the family is just as important.

I conducted an integrated mixed method study to identify and explore relationships among factors that influence the effectiveness of next-generation family leaders and their acquisition of leadership skills, as well as the degree to which they are positively engaged with their work in the family business. There were three phases to the study. The first was a qualitative study that explored factors that differentiated exceptional next-generation family firm leaders from those who were below average. The second phase was a quantitative study of 100 next-generation family leaders informed by the findings of the qualitative study that provided a more precise understanding of the factors that contribute to next-generation leadership effectiveness and work engagement. The third phase was an additional quantitative study that explored the effects of next-generation self-awareness and specific leadership development experiences on their acquisition of leadership skills, motivations for working in the family business, and engagement with their work. Following are some key actions senior and next-generation leaders of family firms can take to address the factors identified in the research as important to next-generation leader development.

Balance a focus on the business with a focus on the family. The study is clear that a positive family climate characterized by open and transparent communication makes it more likely that next-generation leaders will develop the emotional and social intelligence skills that predict leadership effectiveness and provide them with the support they need to practice leadership skills. One important way to facilitate healthy communication in the family is by holding regularly scheduled and well-planned family meetings. Family meetings can be used to help family members work together to create a common vision for the future of the family enterprise, develop ownership goals, create family policies, and provide education on a wide range of topics including communication and leadership skills. The study also provides evidence that business-owning families who communicate effectively help next-generation leaders develop accurate self-awareness, which is critical to the process of learning leadership skills.

Provide next-generation family leaders with challenging work assignments. In addition to family climate, engaging in and valuing challenging work assignments was the other factor in the study that predicted the likelihood that next-generation leaders would assume the personal responsibility that leads to leadership effectiveness and work engagement. This is a particularly important point as next-generation family leaders are often shielded from real responsibility and accountability in the family firm. Family business consultants often recommend that next-generation family members get experience outside the family business to increase the chances they will receive objective feedback on their performance and develop self-confidence. The results of this study suggest that it is the nature of the work experience rather than where it takes place that is the more important factor. The study also suggests that starting early with age-appropriate responsibilities can have positive lifetime effects. The availability of simple chores that can be performed by young next-generation family members to teach them responsibility and expose them to the challenges and rewards of running a family business represents a tremendous advantage for the children of family business owners.

Conduct periodic 360-degree evaluations of all family leaders on a periodic basis. Like so many other studies on leader evaluations, my study confirmed that observer ratings of leader behaviors were significantly more predictive of leadership effectiveness than self-assessments. Senior and next-generation leaders are advised to seek out feedback from employees, peers, and immediate supervisors on a regular basis to stay aware of how others perceive them and to measure their progress in improving leadership effectiveness. Leaders of family firms who are also members of the business-owning family often do not receive accurate feedback on their leadership behaviors. Not only does this impede the development of next-generation leaders, but the study suggests that it can be a major problem for members of the senior generation as well.

Next-generation family business leaders should seek out mentoring relationships. The study showed that mentoring relationships positively affect next-generation leader motivation to succeed in the family business and to engage in challenging work assignments that help them learn leadership skills and positively engage with their work. Mentoring represents another meaningful advantage to next-generation family business leaders when compared to their counterparts in non-family firms. Other studies have shown that next-generation leaders in non-family businesses often do not stay in one position or division long enough to form mentoring relationships. Next-generation leaders of family firms, on the other hand, are more likely to have longer tenures with the family firm and more opportunities to develop mentoring relationships with family or non-family leaders inside or outside the family business. The exceptional leaders in the qualitative phase of the study were almost universal in citing mentoring relationships as important to their development as leaders.

The Final Word

The task of preparing next-generation family members for leadership responsibilities in the family business is too important to leave to chance. The stakes are high for the business, owners, employees, customers, communities served by the family enterprise, and perhaps most of all, for the next generation leaders themselves. I hope my research will serve as a clarion call for business-owning families to provide next-generation family members with opportunities to learn leadership skills through age and experience-appropriate work assignments with genuine responsibility and accountability — and for next-generation leaders to seek out such experiences whether or not they are offered.

Applying the Research Findings and What I Learned from the DM Experience

Teaching. I usually have 50–60 MBA and undergraduate students from all over the world in my family business class at UNC each term. Most come from business-owning families and are thinking deeply about whether or not they should join their family businesses, either immediately after graduation or after gaining experience outside the family firm. More importantly, many are thinking about how they should prepare for the challenge if they do join. The research I completed in the PhD track of CWRU's DM Program has informed the design of my class, the assignments the students are required to complete, the richness of class discussions, and student outcomes from the class. In each instance outlined below, the power of sharing my own research as opposed to simply teaching from a book or relating my own business experience is palpable.

The importance of open and transparent communication in the family informs one of the central tasks of the assigned term paper. Each student is required to interview as many family members as possible to learn about the history of the family firm, family values, how the family communicates, business strategy, and plans for the future of the family firm. The idea behind this assignment is to provide students with an "excuse" for asking mother, father, grandmother, grandfather, aunt, uncle, brother, sister, or cousin about family and family business issues that are often not discussed and assumed to be "off-limits." Students have discovered that they already have ownership they did not know about, reasons behind family business successes and failures, challenges that have been overcome and those that remain, conflicts that have been resolved and those that remain, senior generation hopes and dreams for the future, and a host of other issues that are often viewed as too awkward to discuss. As a result, students, parents, and other relatives involved with the family enterprise often discover that it is not as hard to discuss those issues as they had feared. Relatives often ask to come to class to learn more themselves. Many students have taken on the task of starting the practice of family meeting. Others have gleaned information they need to make their decision on whether or not to join the family firm.

One example is that of a bright young woman from a South American family whose father owned one of the largest privately owned firms in her country. After our first class and a discussion of assignments, she approached me to say that she would regrettably have to drop the class. When I asked her why, she said that she was the oldest of six siblings (all daughters) and that in her culture, women were not encouraged to discuss business and that had been forbidden at the family dinner table. Nonetheless, she expressed a keen interest in the business, so I encouraged her to stay in the class. If her father refused to discuss the business with her, I agreed to help her find another family firm to research for her paper. After several weeks, I was getting concerned that things may not be going so well. To my delight, she showed up at a class about halfway through the term with a wide smile and enthusiastic demeanor. She was anxious to share with me that she had finally worked up the courage to call her father to do the interview and that after five hours of conversation, he had decided to fly to Chapel Hill to engage in deeper discussions about the family firm. That was a good day.

An equally powerful finding of the study that resonates with my students is the finding that a senior generation that leads autocratically is negatively correlated with the development of leadership talent among next-generation family leaders. As many of my students have a mother, father, or other relative who is the entrepreneur who founded or dramatically grew the family firm, the students often recognize the take-charge, make all the rules leadership style that was exercised by many of the senior generation leaders in my study. Rather than allow them to be discouraged by that finding, I have one of the participants in my study come and speak to the class to share with them how he developed a positive relationship with his autocratic father by taking responsibility for his own development and establishing a "business within a business" to gain the leadership experience and self-confidence he needed to develop his own leadership skills. His father had other plans, but this next-generation leader persisted and, in the process, earned his father's respect and confidence. He is now serving as CEO of the entire organization. The students are able to see my research in action and come to understand that while an autocratic senior generation leader may make the task of acquiring leadership skills in the family business more difficult, it is possible to overcome that challenge by taking personal responsibility for their own development.

I also have my students create life plans as my qualitative study revealed that the more effective next-generation family leaders had spent a lot of time in deep reflection about whether or not a career in the family firm would align with their personal life goals. Making that decision is a major reason many students take the class. The quantitative phases of the study further revealed that an "affective" motivation for working in the family firm that reflects a positive emotional connection and strong desire to work for the family firm as a path to personal career fulfillment, as opposed to an obligatory or entitled motivation, has positive effects on next-generation leadership effectiveness, engagement with their work in the family firm, likelihood of taking on challenging work assignments, and even the organizational climate of the firm itself. The research findings lend credibility to the assignment as a practical task, rather than as idealized wishful thinking. Many students write me years later to tell me of the value of the assignment, including when circumstances turn out differently than they had planned or hoped. When unexpected events occur, and they almost always do, the life plan helps them stay anchored in their most important life goals and plan a course correction.

I quickly learned that CWRU pioneered the idea of providing rigorous training for mid-career practitioners who were interested in learning how to do research and wanted to earn a degree beyond a master's degree.

Consulting. One of the things I have learned about family firms is that the issues they face are common, but solutions must be tailored to address the specific circumstances a family firm faces at a particular point in time. Unfortunately, there are no professional standards a family business consultant must meet, although there are some good certification programs that help broaden a family business consultant's perspective and teach facilitation techniques. There are also some very good professional firms that are highly selective in admitting consultants to their practices and which conduct ongoing training to improve knowledge and skills. Some of those firms conduct their own research or encourage their consultants to conduct research. That said, there are still many practitioners in the family business domain who base their consultancies primarily on their own experience. At the same time, there is a growing body of research being conducted by academics as the field continues to grow, some of which is quite helpful to and some of which is fairly disconnected from issues of practical interest to family business practitioners.

Since much of my consulting work involves succession planning and preparing next-generation leaders for leadership responsibilities in family firms, I wanted to explore the literature and do my own research on some relevant gaps in the research on next-gen leadership development. The CWRU program is designed to teach the research skills needed to "bridge the gap" between academics and practitioners. What makes a family firm different from any other form of business organization is the influence the business-owning family has on the strategy, culture, and operation of the firm. While there is a large body of research on leadership development in general, I found that there was gap in the research on how what happens in the family — the family climate — affects next-generation leader development, so that became the focus of my research.

The implications of my research for practice has been extremely valuable to my consulting assignments. Two examples illustrate this point.

In one case, a second-generation family member with strong entrepreneurial skills has grown a local electrical infrastructure construction business into a significant national firm. Two of his sons work in the business and he began preparing for succession over a decade ago.

He was having a hard time letting go, even though he recognized that the firm had grown to a size that it was no longer possible for any one person to make all the decisions. My research findings that the same take-charge autocratic leadership style that had helped him succeed in growing the business was beginning to work against him, his sons, and the organization as he faced the succession challenge resonated strongly with him and the other leaders in the firm. As a result, we were able to develop a multi-year leadership transition plan that reduced his involvement in day-to-day decision making over time, promoted a trusted non-family executive to serve as CEO during an interim period while the sons were developing leadership skills under the non-family executive's mentoring, and develop a team of younger non-family leaders in the firm who would ultimately serve along with the two sons as a leadership team. Part of the plan involved providing the sons with increasing levels of responsibility over time that challenged but did not overwhelm them. The transition is nearly complete after almost nine years of planning and implementation. Not only has the transition taken place seamlessly over time, but the company has more than doubled in size during the process.

In another case, a well-established firm in the printing business with two-second generation (G2) brothers and two third generation (G3) cousins were facing major changes in their industry, which required making some tough decisions. The family owners are very close, supportive, and polite, but they were finding it difficult to discuss and make changes in their business strategy to adapt to new realities. The G3 leaders had some good ideas for moving the business forward but were finding it difficult to be as direct in their communication for fear that they would be perceived as disrespectful to the senior generation. One of the G2 leaders who had managed a highly successful division of the business for many years knew that industry changes had made that division no longer profitable but was fearful of being perceived as having failed the family. The part of my research that demonstrated the importance of open and transparent communication as central to the development of a shared vision for the future of the family business resonated strongly with both generations of family leaders and encouraged them to be more open with each other about the changes that were needed. In just a little over two years, they developed a new strategy for the business, successfully sold one division of the firm, significantly scaled back another, and invested the capital raised in a promising new venture that benefits from the core competencies they developed in the previous businesses. They knew what they needed to do — they just needed some motivation and support in openly discussing and deciding on a course of action.

Conclusion

The DM program at CWRU is the pioneer in engaged scholarship designed to bridge the gap between academics and practitioners. Dr. Kalle Lyytinen once explained that the idea behind the very first universities was to do just that. In my case the program helped me achieve a life-long personal goal and become a more effective teacher and consultant and now it informs my teaching and consulting practice in ways that previously could not have been imagined. More universities should take notice of what is happening in the DM program at CWRU.

Keywords

Family Business, Family Enterprises, Leadership Development, Balance, Generational

About the Author: Stephen P. Miller, DM

Dr. Miller is co-founder of the Family Enterprise Center at UNC Chapel Hill's Kenan-Flagler Business School, and Adjunct Assistant Professor of Organizational Behavior. For 35 years, he served as a senior non-family executive for the Vanderbilt/Cecil family-owned Biltmore Estate in Asheville, N.C. Dr. Miller is president of GenSpan, Inc. In that role, he consults on succession planning, leadership development, and strategy for large family business clients.

Angela C. Crawford

The reason I chose the DM Program at CWRU is that it is a rigorous program with highly respected faculty. The number of doctorate programs entering the market had concerned me because I did not just want three letters after my name. If I were going to invest in this education, it needed to be worth the time and money.

A Journey of Transformation: Rediscovering My Passion

Since the day I earned my undergraduate degree, a framed postcard with the saying "Success is a journey, not a destination" has rested on my bedside table. On my desk at work sits a plaque that is a treasured gift from one of my previous employees that reads, "The journey is the reward." The word journey accurately defines the experience of earning my PhD through the Doctor of Management (DM) program at Case Western Reserve University (CWRU). It has been a journey of personal and professional transformation that is still leading me to unexpected places.

All of us have reasons for pursuing a doctorate in the middle of successful careers. We may articulate these differently, but I find that it comes down to either a mid-life crisis or a burning question we feel compelled to answer. For some, it may be a little of both. However, we tend to talk about our rationale in more practical terms, such as the reasons I gave to people when they asked. I wanted the credentials to be able to teach at the university level when I retired, and I also wanted to earn my degree before I had two children in college who also needed their educations funded. Although in my mind, I knew that the real answer was that I had a burning question.

Over a 20-year career, I traveled throughout the U.S. and the Philippines leading and consulting in contact centers. Wherever I went, I would see frontline employees doing the same job at the same company. Some seemed to love the job like it was their favorite hobby, while others described the work as if it were a prison sentence. How could people doing the same job, in the same location, often being led by the same manager, view their work and the customer so differently? I conducted surveys and focus groups, read practitioner articles, but nothing would explain what I kept encountering. What factors influence frontline employee experiences at work? That was the question that brought me to CWRU, and one that led me to eventually develop a concept called frontline employee passion. I will not discuss the findings here, because they are still in the works for a journal publication. I will say that through the process, I also went through a transformation. During the program, I realized that I had lost my passion for work and, as the saying goes, "researcher heal thyself." I began to discover my own passion through this journey.

The reason I chose the DM program at CWRU is that it is a rigorous program with highly respected faculty. The number of doctorate programs entering the market had concerned me because I did not just want three letters after my name. If I were going to invest in this education, it needed to be worth the time and money.

During the program, I left my corporate job and opened a marketing consulting business. Through the quality of the mixed methods research education I received at CWRU, my clients were amazed at the insights I could share with them about their organizations. The depth of the qualitative and quantitative training allowed me to extract information from data that many executives told me no other consultant had ever shared with them before. I realized at this point that my identity and the value that I brought to my professional career had shifted from practitioner to practitioner-scholar. Although I enjoyed consulting, little did I know that this journey was going to take another turn and bring me into higher education much earlier than expected.

Although my research interest led me to understanding passion from a frontline employee perspective, foundationally, identity was also at the heart of this concept and part of my personal transformation at CWRU. "Passion is more than the experience of strong emotions; it specifically concerns intense positive feelings for activities that are central and meaningful to an individual's self-identity" (Cardon, Wincent, Singh & Drnovsek, 2013: 374). Focusing on identity, identity theorists describe identities as the cognitive schemata we use as internally stored information that serves as a framework for interpreting, experiencing and internalizing the meaning and expectations associated with a role (Stryker & Burke, 2000). What I was going to realize is that my identity was about to change again and, even more importantly, I was going to need to understand how other people view their identities at work.

Since I had been an adjunct instructor in the evenings when I worked, as graduation from CWRU neared, I decided to apply for a full-time teaching job which would also allow me to maintain my consulting business. Near my home was Thomas More College, a Catholic liberal arts school with about 1,200 students. One of my client's husband worked there and she told me that they had an assistant professor job open. I applied and was hired for the fall after I graduated in 2016. At CWRU, my research crossed and intermingled between disciplinary boundaries, which made me an anomaly for universities who wanted highly discipline-specific professors. Not to mention, some schools were definitely opposed to hiring a mid-career, non-traditional PhD

I intend to be at the forefront of this movement — something prior to the PhD I would not have had the knowledge base nor the confidence to do.

with no publication record. At a small liberal arts school, however, I was given the freedom to teach and research across business disciplines. I began teaching undergraduate and graduate students in marketing, management, organizational behavior, and strategy. The students loved that I brought real-life business experience and theory into the classroom. I loved seeing them passionate about learning and their futures.

During my second year, the college decided to move to university status, which meant there became an open position for the founding Dean of the College of Business. I knew that I had never been a Dean, and many people would question my qualifications, including myself. However, throughout my career, my strength was in leading teams into unchartered territory to build and grow new areas. As a person of faith, I also prayed about the opportunity. This stop on my career into the role as Dean was not on my planned journey. The identity of Dean was never something I had aspired to take on as part of my role as a professional.

However, leaders of the college and some senior faculty members began to encourage me to apply. With prayer and faculty support, I decided to interview and was hired for the position. So, with that in the fall of 2018, I became the founding Dean of the College of Business at Thomas More University. We are a small university with a little under 700 Business students majoring in Information Systems, Accounting, and Business Administration. Our size allows me to know the hopes and dreams of many of our students. I have a wall right outside my office that I call the "Wall of Dreams." It has their photos and dreams they share about what they want for their futures proudly displayed.

In spring of 2017, when it was announced that I would be the Dean of the College of Business, I received about the same proportion of notes and phone calls of congratulations as I did condolences and questions about why I would leave a successful career to become part of the "administration." Fortunately, my exceptional qualitative training, thanks to Drs. Richard Boland and Kalle Lyytinen at CWRU, prepared me well to listen carefully and understand people at a deeper level. In my mind, I formulated two questions, similar to how I develop research questions, "What are the lived experiences of faculty members?" and "What are the lived experiences of successful Deans at teaching universities?" Of course, this was no official study. It is just an example of how my mindset became transformed through the CWRU DM program.

As part of my learning process, I interviewed faculty members who would be part of the College of Business, asking them to share with me specific examples of what they enjoyed most and least about their jobs. I also asked them a time when they felt like the university, and then their department, was at its very best. Times of change are very stressful, and we were in the middle of one of those situations, so it was beautiful to see the hope that began to appear in many of their eyes. Next, I attended the Accreditation Council for Business Schools and Programs (ACBSP) conference in June of that year and then the Dean's conference in November. I kept my notebook handy asking questions to evoke rich stories about successes and failures from Deans, faculty members, and chairpersons. Again, this was not an official research project. However, it was immensely valuable to me in learning my role. Of course, I also listened carefully to the words and phrases our acting provost and president used.

Through all of this, I began to hear and see a pattern of an "us" versus "them," with faculty using language such as "the administration." Social identity and in-group versus out-group membership, which I had learned about seemed to now be at play. These themes I was seeing were reinforced one day when a colleague of mine who left academia called me and said "Hey, why don't you come back to consulting where there are people who like you, and you can actually make money, instead of getting paid almost nothing to be on the dark side of the university and likely one of the most hated people on campus." I laughed it off, but I understood what he was saying. It was a mental model that he had built that led him to ultimately leave a tenured role at a university. The good news is that by using an investigative approach like this as I was entering a new role, I believe that I have been able to begin to bridge the divide between our faculty members and administration.

Certainly, it may be easier for me as a Dean who also teaches two classes each semester. However, taking this qualitative approach to learning a new role has helped me find ways to build common ground between meeting the needs of faculty members and the needs of the university. The truth is that there are common goals between faculty members and administrators if we look and listen carefully. For instance, at our university, we all care about our students, and we want to see the university be maintained and grow. Just like administrators, faculty members want to be valued for the expertise that they bring to work each day. And just like faculty members, administrators want to know that they are making a difference.

Of course, there will always be challenges, and I have only scratched the surface in my learning. However, our school allows all full-time faculty to anonymously provide feedback about their Dean's performance, and although I was nervous about reading it, I was pleased to see the results this year. Two of the numerous kind comments below reinforced that my qualitative approach to learning this new role has paid off so far and that maybe I was getting closer to regaining my passion for work:

> *"Dean Crawford sets mission and vision and includes faculty in creating the goals and strategies for the College. She is very supportive of faculty and assists in faculty development and new programs. She encourages faculty to engage with the*

community and connects students with the business world. She takes pride in faculty achievements and helps faculty to continue to increase subject knowledge and reach their goals."

"Dr. Crawford is passionate about the college and the students in it."

As I have explained, my degree from CWRU was instrumental in preparing me to take on this role as a faculty member and administrator. The knowledge that I gained has provided me the ability to bridge what many believe is a wide chasm between the administration and faculty. I hold my identity as a scholar very close to me, which also allows me to relate and understand our faculty members in ways that I believe helps me to be more successful in my role. In the high winds of change and uncertainty in higher education, my 20 years of practitioner experience provides me with the understanding and creativity to approach this new administrative role in unique ways.

At Thomas More University, our mission is to "challenge students of all faiths to examine the meaning of life, their place in the world, and their responsibility to others." The transformation from a practitioner, to a scholar, to administrator has been an exercise in integrating and blending new identities in just a few short years. It has also taken me on a personal and professional journey of finding my place in the world that allows me to live out my passion for helping others achieve their dreams. Although I still don't see the final destination of this journey, I know that I am well prepared for any unexpected path.

Keywords
Frontline Employee Experience, Identity, Passion, Social Identity

About the Author: Angela C. Crawford, PhD
Dr. Crawford is on a mission to help people and organizations discover and live out their passion. She has spent over 25 years in designing and enhancing customer and employee experiences. Her career spans executive leadership, marketing, research, operations, and sales.

As Dean of the College of Business at Thomas More University, Dr. Crawford enjoys teaching MBA and undergraduate students; while also maintaining her consulting and executive coaching where she helps organizations and people become the best version of themselves. Dr. Crawford earned her BBA in Marketing and Management from the University of Cincinnati, MBA from Cleveland State University, and PhD. from Case Western Reserve University. She lives in Northern Kentucky with her family, where she also serves as a hospice volunteer and church board member.

Cory A. Campbell

The experiences in pursuing my doctoral degree were so much more than I had ever expected they would be. I never anticipated having such a tight-knit cohort based on the residency model. In addition to truly learning to think beyond what is possible, I learned so much about myself and built some amazing relationships, which will last a lifetime.

Beyond Academia: One Practitioner Scholar's Approach to Transform the Future of Accountancy as Well as the Future of Higher Education Policy

The Doctor of Management (DM) program at Case Western Reserve University (CWRU) has truly enabled me to think beyond what is possible. Currently, I am a tenure-track faculty member at Indiana State University where I teach courses in Accounting Information Systems (AIS) and Governmental and Non-Profit Accounting. However, the practitioner-scholar mindset embedded throughout the CWRU doctoral program has enabled me to bridge the gap between academia and practice, thus creating a platform to make a meaningful contribution through research, advocating for the accounting profession, and providing some consulting services to an organization charged with serving the underserved in higher education.

The Journey to CWRU

My career path as an entrepreneur diverged because of the recession spurred by subprime mortgage lending. As markets tightened, I transitioned my career path from an entrepreneur to the world of finance and administration in the higher education sector. As an administrator in higher education, I served as the Chief Financial Officer at small private liberal arts college and as Associate Director for Financial Reporting for the Indiana University School of Medicine. In these various professional roles, I relied heavily upon Information Systems in order to ensure the completeness, accuracy, and integrity of both financial and non-financial data. As a practitioner, I could experience first-hand how various projects integrated the transformational power of technology with AIS, but my passion for research in AIS is rooted in my experience of applying to become a licensed Certified Public Accountant (CPA). After successfully completing the CPA exam, I applied for state licensure and was aghast to learn that the state initially did not view my professional experience in Management Information Systems (MIS) as applicable to accounting and that I needed to provide additional evidence of my experience in order to gain state licensure.

I did just that and became hooked on the research after an article published in *MIS Quarterly* which discussed the impact of information technology on internal controls from an accountancy perspective satisfied the licensing board. As a newly licensed CPA, I became intrigued by the power of research in affecting real-world outcomes. That inspiration, coupled with having taught classes as an adjunct instructor led me to the doctoral program at CWRU as I found my calling in academia.

> To be successful as an academic, one needs to excel in teaching, research, and service. Having a practitioner-scholar mindset can create valuable service to the university in novel ways.

The year-one Fall residency was my first trip to CWRU. I made a commitment to CWRU based on the school's credentials and academic ranking as the DM program was simply the best Association to Advance Collegiate Schools of Business (AASCB) accredited school that allowed some flexibility for working adults. The experiences in pursuing my doctoral degree were so much more than I had ever expected they would be. I never anticipated having such a tight-knit cohort based on a residency model. In addition to truly learning to think beyond what is possible, I learned so much about myself and built some amazing relationships, which will last a lifetime.

Life as an Academic

Indiana State University is an ideal match for me based on my teaching interests, institutional demographics, and the proximity to my home. I absolutely love the flexibility of my schedule, as my typical teaching load is 3 classes in fall and 3 classes in spring with face-to-face classes that meet twice per week plus one online class; an ideal schedule for a practitioner scholar who aspires to engage in different things! I enjoy teaching and believe that students benefit from my experience in the real world that I can bring into the classroom. Real world stories from the administrative lens of higher education or stories from the years spent in the import industry are great ways to connect with students. Personal accounts from dealing with labor strikes by the dockworkers in California, customer's filing bankruptcy, and employee fraud bring the textbook topics to life in order to enrich the student experience. Another way to enrich the student experience is through redesigning an online class with the help of a course designer thanks to an institutional grant. I have found that the principles of what I learned in that course redesign process have been very beneficial in face to face class setting as well because of the thoughtful reflection about learning outcomes and how to align those with assignments has made me a better teacher.

Another institutional grant has helped me try to embed a service-learning component into my classes. Many students in an Accounting Information Systems course will learn to visualize accounting information and produce dashboards that they can use to highlight their skills to prospective employers.

For the 2020 academic year, I am developing new courses in accounting analytics — a gap that many institutions are scrambling to plug as the profession is demanding different skillsets. One course will include more advanced skills and projects on text-mining, process automation, and advanced visualization. The second course will be an introductory AIS course that will integrate Excel and Tableau skills with some accounting problems. I was inspired to add an introductory accounting analytics course after providing feedback on a new textbook forthcoming from McGraw Hill that is written by Dr. Vernon Richardson, a member of my dissertation committee. In addition to teaching and curriculum, other major aspects of life in academia include research and service.

Keeping an active research agenda has been easy considering that I had an amazing dissertation committee including Drs. Tim Fogarty (chair), Kalle Lyytinen, and Phil Cola from CWRU and Vernon Richardson from the University of Arkansas. These scholars really pushed me, so I am grateful to be working on projects with each of my committee members. My qualitative research study (Campbell & Fogarty, 2018) highlights the challenges with the adoption of information systems technology in higher education. Two separate quantitative studies from my dissertation work on the intersection between technology and finance in higher education have been sent to various journals. Dr. Fogarty and I submitted a paper on the perceptions of information quality from the Chief Business Officer perspective while Drs. Lyytinen, Cola, and I submitted a paper, which utilizes an analytics maturity index for institutions of higher learning. There should be additional publications from the data collected for my dissertation. Dr. Richardson and I will be working on a study that pairs perceptions of the Chief Financial Officer with the perceptions of Information Technology for approximately 200 institutions. Additionally, since we have a data maturity index for three years, a longitudinal study is on the horizon.

I am interested in emerging technology and have done some research into various topics such as blockchain. The Accounting Association of America (AAA) really liked a proposal submitted to a 2018 Blockchain Forum in San Francisco, CA, so much that it morphed into a featured conference presentation. This was an exciting opportunity, but a two-hour presentation requires a lot of content! I collaborated on this project with one of my colleagues from the CWRU DM program, Dr. Dijo Alexander. We were also able to make a condensed version of this presentation at the World Continuous Audit Reporting Forum hosted at Rutgers University. Presenting at Rutgers, a leading institution in AIS doctoral programs, was a great opportunity to build my network as I meet new colleagues there, which spurn new research opportunities. Networking at this conference lead to a project on the adoption of data analytics into the accounting information systems curriculum based on the push-pull dynamic between practice and the AACSB accrediting body.

The profession is really changing quickly due to emerging technology and because of my interest in this area, I have been tapped as a journal reviewer. Between the *Journal of Information Systems* and *Accounting Horizons*, I have peer-reviewed seven different articles on topics ranging from blockchain to inter-organizational relationships to big data. Currently, I have two papers under review and five projects in various draft stages. Ultimately, my research focus in Accounting Information Systems aims to increase financial transparency because the future of the accountancy profession lies at the intersection of finance, technology, and information. To be successful as an academic, one needs to excel in teaching, research, and service. Having a practitioner-scholar mindset can create valuable service to the university in novel ways. As a practitioner scholar, service work for the university can be aimed at the accounting profession or seeking to make a difference with higher education policy.

Influencing the Future of Accountancy

Working as a practitioner scholar has been rewarding beyond my world in academia. I have made numerous presentations to the Indiana CPA society on various types of emergent technologies including big data, blockchain, and cybersecurity. CPA's are required to earn 120 hours of continuing education every three years. Speaking at continuing education workshops for CPAs on these various emergent technologies has been a lot work, but it is rewarding to be recognized at the forefront of such issues. I find much of this coming full circle in a very powerful way as this invariably creates opportunities in the classroom as well as with research.

For example, the state CPA society asked me to speak at a Business and Industry conference on cybersecurity. A 75-minute presentation to a room full of accountants on cybersecurity forced me to excel my rudimentary understanding of cybersecurity in order to become better informed. Cybersecurity is increasingly important to accountants.

A joint statement about the future of the CPA exam describes cybersecurity as a key skill for accountants of the future. Delving into this area as a speaker and as the chairperson for an INCPA Society Cybersecurity conference, I have insights that I can leverage as a researcher. As states are adopting laws on biometrics or laws more restrictive than what Europe instilled with General Data Protection Regulation (GDPR), I am poised to think about the technological and ethical questions that would be interesting research topics.

Additionally, I have been able to serve as a content expert for the American Institution of Certified Public Accountants (AICPA) hosting all day workshops in different parts of the country. During the fall of 2019, I facilitated blockchain workshops in Chicago and San Diego. I anticipate being able to host 10–12 workshops for the AICPA annually. I have been an invited speaker for a podcast as a thought leader for the finance and accounting profession for *Go Beyond Disruption*, which provides insights on emerging technology and digital transformation.

Accounting, dubbed as the language of business, has become highly dependent on data. In fact, I tell my students that it is no longer "Debits and Credits" but rather "Debits, Credits, and Data." Accountants have to be stewards of data — which include an understanding of IT governance and cybersecurity. Data analytics, the Internet of Things, robotics process automation (RPA), and artificial intelligence (AI) are the future of business so we need to build skillsets that are adaptable to changing technology. *The Big Four* are embracing changes with technology and upskilling their workforces. Forbes suggests key skills for the future include technology skills, communication skills, and critical thinking skills. Critical thinking as introduced from real-world concepts to demonstrate how analytics adds value to business and how the data flows through the organization are skills required to be successful in the future (Forbes, 2017).

In a practitioner piece on emerging technology in accounting, I suggest that big data analytics and AI may do the number crunching and analysis, allowing accountants to focus on higher-level tasks. This is great because the breadth and scope of what accountants do continues to widen (Campbell, 2019). The promise of big data is transforming the way we do business and is impacting most other parts of our lives (Campbell, 2019). Working as an advocate for the profession has been an invigorating way for me to provide service to the university where my primary role is a tenure track professor.

Influencing Higher Education Policy

I have been fortunate to serve as a financial consultant to Complete College America. The noble purpose of this organization is to advance higher education by closing achievement gaps. My role is to provide support with strategic finance. In this role, I provide guidance for financial reporting and operational budgeting. I am the liaison to the Board of Trustees for fiscal matters. In December of 2019, I attended the annual convening meeting for the Complete College America in Phoenix, AZ. This event brings together leaders from public universities (e.g., Presidents and Provosts) around the country with leaders from the states (e.g., governors, the commission for higher education) to work collaboratively for greater innovation, to move evidence-based strategies to scale, and to make stronger policy in order to have the largest impact possible for students.

My relationship with Complete College America has created research opportunities to make a positive impact on education policy. Dr. Phil Cola and I are working on a project for the Commission of Higher Education Policy for West Virginia, which is, supported the Michael and Susan Dell Foundation. The purpose of the study is to explore the return on investment for implementation of co-requisite support — which is a model for implementing development education (e.g., remedial Math and English) in a new way that removes barriers to student success and increases gateway course completion. We are hopeful to present this work to other foundations whose goals are embedded in improving higher education and providing equitable opportunities for students of different socio-economic and demographic backgrounds.

What Lies Ahead

My goal going into the program at CWRU was to become a tenure track professor at Indiana State University because of my personal connection to the institution. The fact that I have been able to do just that while becoming a nationally recognized expert by the accounting profession in emerging technology and working closely with an organization focused solely on improving college completion has been an amazingly rewarding journey.

One could argue the biggest challenge for the accounting profession of tomorrow is dealing with companies and technologies that do not yet exist today (Campbell, 2019). Merging research and service activities has created a professional niche that I hope to continue to build upon and leverage. My hope is that this will continue to serve me for years to come.

Keywords

Emerging Technology, Experiential Learning, Financial Consultant, Higher Education Policy, Co-Requisite Support

About the Author: Cory A. Campbell, PhD

Dr. Campbell is an Assistant Professor of Accounting at Indiana State University. He earned his PhD from the Weatherhead School of Management at Case Western Reserve University. He is licensed as a Certified Public Accountant (CPA), Chartered Global Management Accountant (CGMA), and a Certified Fraud Examiner (CFE). His teaching and research interests lie at the intersection between accounting and technology. Dr. Campbell facilitates CPE workshops for the Indiana CPA Society on various emerging technologies and has been a subject matter expert for the AIPCA on blockchain technology and cybersecurity.

"*Great things in business are never done by one person. They're done by a team of people.*"

Steve Jobs

Connector

Building collaborations to
change the environment as an
institutional entrepreneur

Patricia J. Mintz

As a result of the DM Program, I continue to ask questions and make inquiries in unique ways to develop research proposals and grant applications with appropriate literature review.

Personal Transformation: Discovering the Power of Practitioner-Scholarship

As I crossed the stage with my family to accept my Doctor of Management Degree (DM awarded on May 18, 2003) at Case Western Reserve University (CWRU), I realized completing the DM degree launched a brand new segment of my professional and personal life.

I completed the requirements of this unique, innovative academic program at the doctoral level of which I will never forget. After graduation, I used my leadership approach to create a collaboration with faculty, staff, and administrators as I turned my full workplace attention to being the Dean of Business, Math, and Technology at Cuyahoga Community College (Tri-C). Reading, writing, and academic discoveries became a daily engagement that I would incorporate in discussions with people as I walked the hallways in the classroom buildings, creating impromptu discussions about academic courses, course requirements, and resources at Tri-C in the Fall Semester of 2003 and beyond.

Today as an education consultant, I continue to use ethnography as an engagement tool in the educational community. I learned that I could observe students or staff working in open access computer labs in a more specific ways to guide my work to design the labs. I seek advice and support from the staff and faculty who teach and work in the computer labs. I use my ethnography skills to create the descriptions needed to support improved tutoring and written communication using computer resources. I use my observation skills gained through ethnographic research in all meetings that I attend at work or in the community.

The skills of ethnographic observation focus me on the development of each individual student that I might meet. I observe the individual's willingness to make eye contact while sharing ideas, telling a story or making a request. Students, faculty and staff may often bring requests and ideas that can be shared and implemented for all to benefit.

I established groups of five to seven staff and faculty members in the areas of business, mathematics, and technology. I encouraged each group to meet and discuss needs at least once a month. I received a summary report for determining student engagement and future common needs for more interactive learning experiences.

I learned from student comments that utilization of computers and software were not enough to be successful in learning mathematics. I chose to spend time in the open access computer labs and presented myself as a Mathematics specialist. I found that working with students who had the courage to ask questions provides the learning environment that models ways to grow and expand personal understanding.

As a consultant, I know that transforming qualitative information strengthens my ability to describe the work of faculty. Classroom visitations and faculty evaluations become personally descriptive for the faculty member. My visit to a classroom is expanded to include descriptions of student engagement with an ethnography approach. I watch and describe how a student takes notes, follows the professor's explanation, and asks specific questions. I admire and comment about any instructor's ability to make their students comfortable to speak up and ask a question. I have always believed that a student who asks a question in a class discussion is also asking for at least five students who were not comfortable to ask for themselves.

I decided to informally offer ten to fifteen minute meetings with any faculty member (full time or adjunct) to discuss their needs for innovative approaches. Gathering qualitative data allows me to use my research techniques to determine the best way to proceed to support students and gain more funding for expanded support services.

Using the quantitative approaches to evaluate the effectiveness of academic programs allows me to ask substantive questions of other academic administrators. I present the data and evaluations to my colleagues at multiple campuses at college wide meetings. This college wide discussion creates common knowledge and understanding that supports the student learning experience and welcomes students to seek information and data from faculty and departments that support the student's chosen degree program.

As a result of the DM Program, I continue to ask questions and make inquiries in unique ways to develop research proposals and grant applications with appropriate literature review. Librarian support from Tri-C and CWRU continues to lead me to resources that provide an extraordinary collection of books, articles,

The six founding faculty members for the DM program . . . established the expectation that graduates would always continue to search for excitement with new ideas and academic approaches in their future endeavors.

and conference possibilities. Through OhioLINK, a full network of resources that is coordinated for use by all students, faculty, staff, and graduates of colleges and universities in Ohio, each librarian is able to guide requests and expand possible choices for each researcher. The book and/or article that I acquire through OhioLINK is a resource that I continue to use in my leadership roles in academics and the nonprofit sector.

Classmates and professors continue to provide personal transformation advice that helps me clarify the use of my expanded knowledge in academic leadership administrative roles in my career at Tri-C. I learned to establish a demeanor that empowers students, faculty, and staff to ask for help and support that is positive and focused on growth and new possibilities.

This leadership philosophy clearly established my desire to interview for new positions both in and out of current responsibilities. Reorganization and searching for academic leadership talent over the next several years gave me the opportunity to be promoted and hired as the Dean of Academic Affairs and then the Vice President of Student Success for Tri-C. I created specific objectives for each of the departments that reported to me, always looking for individuals who wanted to lead on their campus and set the expectations for the students that sought tutoring and testing services. Often, adjunct faculty were supported by also tutoring and keeping a focus on student engagement. I retired from Tri-C on May 1, 2011, from this college wide academic administrator position, to begin new adventures in the greater Cleveland community.

I volunteered to help establish the Robert L. Lewis Academy of Scholars Program at Tri-C. I realized that a decision to retire is not necessarily a decision to completely disconnect from an educational institution that I have served for 27 years.

The Scholars Program requires an application from a student that has a particular interest in social justice and civic responsibility. The applications are reviewed and offers to enroll in the required honors course for social justice is extended to the interested students.

Once a student enrolls in the Honors Social Justice Course, the student becomes an enthusiastic community-based researcher. I watch and support students with ideas for completing community-based project for change and innovation.

During my doctoral studies in the DM program, I was selected for a nonprofit fellowship that was supported through the David and Lucile Packard Foundation. I realize that these additional seminars on Thursdays at each residency set the stage for my transition to building nonprofit management leadership skills. Because of the fellowship, I was engaged in a collaboration through The Mandel Center for Nonprofit Organizations and the Weatherhead School of Management. The fellowship sessions provided a series of opportunities to meet nonprofit management leaders in the community.

Because I live in Cleveland, Ohio, I have the opportunity to join in the discussions and research presentations at the Nonprofit Research Affinity Group led by Dr. Paul Salipante at Case Western Reserve University. I continue to take advantage of the 90-minute lunch meetings to meet current DM students and participate in discussions about the research being developed and completed. The discussions are always open and lively, and each attendee is encouraged to offer ideas to a current DM student presenter.

Using history as an initial framework for growth and development within nonprofit organizations, I continue to learn from the work of Dr. David Hammack, Professor of History at CWRU and expert in the nonprofit sector. Dr. Hammack has recently retired from his full-time role, however I have had many opportunities to participate in lunch supported gatherings that are specifically centered on the role and importance of nonprofit organizations in the United States and around the world. I was challenged by Dr. Hammack to consider how a nonprofit organization is functional and valued in the general community. I consider the trusteeship role a major contribution to the strength and growth of a nonprofit organization.

I continue to be impressed by the story of Alexis de Tocqueville, a French Diplomat who traveled to America because of his interest in democracy and the equality of conditions that allow for the development of volunteer organizations. I believe that groups of individuals come together and decide to form an organization that is open to volunteers who share a common purpose or problem that needs to be addressed.

I currently serve in the role of trustee for two different nonprofit organizations. I know the responsibility and communication with other trustees on a board must be completed efficiently and effectively to move any organization toward the completion of plans for fulfilling the mission, financial growth, and succession planning that have been defined through the collaborative discussion of the members of the board of trustees.

The research work of Dr. Mark Granovetter (e.g., the Strength of Weak Ties) affects my volunteer work on nonprofit boards. I use his idea to communicate needs of an individual organization that takes the time to build a network of community members that know the needs of a nonprofit organization and can consider what contributions are viable. This is especially true with a nonprofit organization that creates and supports housing options for individuals with special needs. I serve as a trustee for this organization. I chair the Mission Committee that is currently working to define the expected needs in the next five years as individuals with the support of parents and/or guardians seek housing in the community that can support individual specific special needs.

I recently learned that the members of the Mission Committee each had a specific person or family member that brought them to the committee table to learn what is needed for high quality housing. I believe that these committee members will take a leadership role to make contacts and connections to support the work of special needs housing that is community based. I continue to share information and resources that I personally know will support changes and resolve challenges.

I chose to lead this committee because I can use my practitioner-scholar skills to define the collaborations that are required. I work with the Cuyahoga County Board of Developmental Disabilities and the support administrator that coordinates the authoring of an annual Individual Service Plan for each resident with special needs. I have a personal passion for this work because my adult son is a resident of a home for individuals with special needs.

I also serve as a trustee for an organization that serves to strengthen families in both the Jewish and general communities in Northeast Ohio. As a trustee, I have the opportunity to participate in communal responsibility, social justice initiatives, and overall enhance every individual's ability to thrive in the community. I continue to support the commitment to help individuals face challenges with confidence.

Volunteer trusteeship allows me to collaborate with the executive leaders of organizations. I emphasize the need to define a specific role for each trustee or committee member that ensures their comfort level and engagement. A dear friend and mentor once advised me if others do not agree at times, it is always easier to ask for forgiveness instead of asking for permission to take on specific leadership roles. I want leadership to be forthright with data and specific goals that are fulfilled by the organization's hired officers and staff. I believe that this can happen when people feel welcome and continue to engage with a needed program and its resources.

I have transitioned to a consultant role since my retirement from Tri-C. I consult as it allows me great flexibility. I continue to maintain my contact with the DM program. I look for ways to give back emotionally and through financial resources that are controlled directly by the DM Program.

The six founding faculty members for the DM program (Drs. John Aram, Richard Boyatzis, Bo Carlsson, Jagdip Singh, Paul Salipante and Richard Boland) established the expectation that graduates would always continue to search for excitement with new ideas and academic approaches in their future endeavors.

This is exactly my expectation as I continue to stay associated with the Weatherhead School DM program at CWRU. I have recently learned that several of the founding faculty members have accepted leadership roles to review curriculum, course requirements, and potential directions to encourage enrollment over the next 20 years.

I will continue to learn and grow my knowledge base along with both current students and graduates as I look forward to the 25th anniversary of the DM Program in April 2020.

Keywords
Academic Leadership, Nonprofit Trusteeship, Ethnography, Qualitative Information, Quantitative Information, Weak Ties, Education Consultant

About the Author: Patricia J. Mintz, DM

Dr. Mintz currently works as an independent education consultant and a nonprofit strategic strategist in the greater Cleveland, Ohio area. After completing a bachelors and master's degree in mathematics, she taught mathematics to more than 3,000 students in middle school, high school, and community colleges in Ohio, New Jersey, and Michigan. She moved to administrative roles by accepting a position as Director of Faculty Development at Cuyahoga Community College, which was her first administrative role. Dr. Mintz progressed at Cuyahoga Community College to become the Dean of Business, Math and Technology, and then the Dean of Academic Affairs and finally served as the Vice President of Student Success. Overall, she had the honor and privilege of serving Cuyahoga Community College for 27 years before transitioning to consulting. She has a husband and two grown children that continue to receive a great deal of her attention.

Nancy Koury King

I know this undertaking would not have been possible without my DM education. It was natural for me to network and reach out to academic resources from different disciplines as I had learned to do in the DM program.

A Practitioner-Scholar's Journey to Writing "Fired: How to Manage Your Career in the Age of Uncertainty"

Introduction, Problem of Practice, and Personal Interest

> *"I felt betrayed. I was raised that hard work, being loyal, and treating others with respect would be rewarded. That didn't pan out. You can be doing the best job and be successful, but for reasons beyond your control you can lose your job. The counselors say look at this as an opportunity. I can tell you it's not an opportunity."* — Joe

Have you ever experienced an employer-driven job loss? I have, and it was devastating. When I lost my job, I received dozens of calls from supportive friends and colleagues. I welcomed the emotional and the job search support. What surprised me was how many of them said to me, "You don't know this Nancy, but that happened to me." They assured me that I was not alone and told me their stories of how they lost their jobs. I found it comforting to know that people I held in high esteem had also faced this loss.

I was shocked as well. Like many of the people I eventually interviewed, I believed if you were loyal, did a good job, and worked hard, you would be rewarded. Like them, I never really considered the relevance and risks of employment at will. I started thinking about their stories with my "DM" hat on and began to notice the patterns. Then I realized there was a bigger story to be told and decided to write a book.

"Dr. Nancy King's research on how to anticipate and survive being let go from a job provides a valuable service to all of those working in today's insecure workplaces." — Dr. Jone Pearce, Professor, University of California Irvine

I sought the advice of Dr. Paul Salipante, who recommended that I talk with Dr. Jone Pearce of the University of California, Irvine. Dr. Pearce encouraged me to pursue my study and shared that most research on job loss are from the employer's point of view and that very little data exists from the employee's point of view. Ironically, the topic was also a personal concern for Dr. Pearce as a family member's company was planning a major layoff and they were hoping the family member would not be affected. "It is everywhere," I thought.

> In true practitioner-scholar form, I wrote a book that was grounded in research yet accessible to the public.

Whether it is called a layoff, reduction in force, being let go, or being fired, job loss is surprising common in our world. According to the Bureau of Labor Statistics, 21,888,000 people in this country were discharged or laid off in 2018. Job uncertainty is the new normal. In addition, from my own observations and research, most people are not prepared for or even cognizant of this possibility. Now I had an important message to share! But how?

Methods

To answer this question, I re-read my first- and second-year research projects and qualitative research books from the DM program. I began outlining a research design and interview questionnaire. I would use inductive methods rather than view the data through the lens of a theory. It was important for me to hear their stories directly and unfiltered. "The qualitative research interview attempts to understand the world from the subject's point of view, to unfold the meaning of peoples' experiences, to uncover their lived world prior to scientific explanations," (Kvale,1996, p. 1).

I interviewed 65 individuals who had been fired, laid off, or had their job eliminated. I listened to several others who shared the story of someone they knew who was let go. I also triangulated my research with stories of firings in the news.

Sadly, though fortunate for my research, finding people to interview was easy. Through personal and professional networking, I found the first set of respondents. They were eager to talk about their experiences. For example, here is a quote from one subject describing his firing.

> *"I call this 'the moment' — both my manager and depart-ment manager showed up at my door with a fistful of papers. Time actually seemed to slow. My department manager was smiling ear to ear — the smile of a long-sought victory — while my direct manager was sullen. I was told that if I didn't sign these papers, I would not receive my final pay and some other 'benefits' and that it would all work out the same anyhow, so for the betterment of my family I should sign. My face was flush with embarrassment. I, a hardworking, honest guy, was being fired."* — Don

I shared these initial interview notes with Dr. Raymond Noe, Fisher College of Business at The Ohio State University. He commented on the rich and compelling stories and urged me to keep going.

From here, I asked people I interviewed to refer me to others they knew who might be willing to be interviewed. "You should talk to so-and-so" was a common response. No one declined to be interviewed. In addition, when I would tell people what my book was about, almost invariably, either they would convey to me they personally or someone they knew had just gone through a job loss.

The research took place over a period of five years. It was difficult to stop the data collection phase of this project as I continued to identify new participants with powerful stories. To this day, I am asked to hear people's stories and I keep a file of them for "the next book."

My DM education provided me the skills to code and organize my interviews. After data gathering, I read and reread each interview several times. I used open coding to identify commonalities and themes in the participants' stories. I repeated this process to capture themes as comprehensively as possible (Boyatzis, 1998). I then arranged my notes to put together passages of interviews with similar themes. I also organized my notes by the questions on my interview guide. I did not use a coding software program; rather I coded all the interviews manually. Doing so helped me more deeply absorb and understand their meanings. I reflected often on my writing and research and acknowledged in the book that I had been on both sides of the firing line. To guard against bias as much as possible, I used my interviewees' own words.

For me, the research was the easy part. Interviewing people who took me along their journey was a privilege and a window into the world of struggles people who have lost jobs encounter. The thematic analysis and coding were energizing. I encountered many themes I did not expect as well as found ample evidence for those I did.

The Journey

In case you are wondering, I am fully aware that writing about being fired could be construed as a career-limiting move. Not many people want to be associated with the word 'fired' (current president notwithstanding). I could tell, even though he did not say so directly, that a dear friend and fellow DM classmate was worried about me and the potential negative association of writing this book.

The book is intentionally and boldly about the predictors, impact, and recovery of losing a job from the employee's, not the employer's, perspective. It sheds light on today's employment practices and the imbalance of power associated with employment at will. In addition, it questions the commonly held belief that if you work hard you will be rewarded.

So, where did I get the nerve? And how did I summon the drive to complete my book? It would have been so easy to just continue the interviews; there were abundant opportunities to listen to more stories. However, I had to stop. I had told so many people I was writing a book, I felt I had to finish it. I owed it to those I interviewed and those who helped me. These stories needed to be told.

Finally, I made a New Year's resolution to stop the research and write the book. The agony began when I started organizing the work into chapters and actually writing. Admittedly, I struggled the most with finding my voice — what tone should I take? How much advice should I add? And mostly, should I attempt to write and publish for academic publication and use or for the general public?

In true practitioner-scholar form (Salipante & Aram, 2003), I wrote a book that was grounded in research yet accessible to the public. I presented my findings along major themes with a chapter devoted to each of them. I titled the chapters using plays on the word fired or words associated with it such as "Where There's Smoke there's fire," "You're not Fireproof," and "Burn Notice." I thought Dr. Paul Salipante would like that. At the end of each chapter, I summarized a few takeaways for the reader. The book, which I self-published in December 2017, is entitled *Fired: How to Manage Your Career in the Age of Job Uncertainty.* After so many years of work, I could not endure a search for publisher.

Possible Audiences
This book and its findings have the potential to benefit and inform a variety of audiences. Obviously, it can bring comfort and practical advice for those who have lost a job. One reader said, "Thank you for writing about something that is so secretive in peoples' lives." For those dependent on full time work and benefits, the book provides a warning and advice for handling the consequences of employment at will. Another reader wrote, "I wish I had read this book before I was forced to resign."

The book has also touched managers and human resources professionals who want to improve the culture and employee engagement of their workforce. One manager encouraged her leadership students to read my book before they ever need to fire someone so that they would be more sensitive. Another manager said her organization's leaders read my book in order to sensitively plan for a reduction in force. Outplacement firms and career coaches may also find this an appropriate resource for their clients. Further, college career centers, career coaches, and outplacement firms could use the findings of this study to inform their own practices as well as directly help their students and clients.

Findings
So, what did I learn? Or as one DM classmate would say, "What are the takeaways?" The research offered several important and practical findings. Here are just a few of them:

"I just knew she wanted to bring in her own team."

First, the biggest predictors of job loss in this study were getting a new boss/leader and starting a new job, which most often involves a new supervisor. In fact, more than half of those I interviewed had either a new job or a new supervisor or both before being let go. These predictors can have implications for anyone working in an organization.

"How do I go from outstanding to terminated?"

Second, being a loyal employee, doing a great job, and working hard did not insulate people from being let go. Subjects in my study had received praise, excellent performance reviews, promotions, and even awards. Politics and personalities played a much bigger role. It seems without some sort of protection or contract, no one is fireproof.

"It's like a divorce."
"If your job is your identity, and you lose your job, who are you?"

Third, losing a job has a profound emotional, social, and financial impacts. Subjects were able to describe feelings of loss, depression, anger, fear, and shame. Many not only lost their income and financial security, but they lost a set of friends and a social network that had become a fixture in their lives. Even their own identity was affected.

> *"We live in a beautiful home, but I realize it all can become a garage sale tomorrow. I don't even want to improve our home, thinking it's not permanent. I'd be spending my energies building something for another man I don't even know."*
> *"Did I grow? If anything, I grew with a level of suspiciousness and distrust that was never in me before. I don't know that that will heal anyone."*

Fourth, the interviewees reported being different after their job loss. Many voiced a new distrust for employers that was not there prior to their job loss. While they still wanted to do a good job, they were no longer willing to become as engaged and sacrifice as much for their companies. They also reported that less of their identity was wrapped up in their job and company.

"I learned no one helps you but you. It doesn't matter that you had great evaluations, that you were there 27 years, that you won an international award. None of that matters. It doesn't matter. What matters is letting the boss do what she wants. I learned my lesson. Now I know. Now I know you have to look out for yourself."

Fifth, the interviewees described their new understanding of loyalty and trust. They no longer believed that the company and their supervisor would look out for them because they were loyal and did a good job. The interviewees transferred the loyalty they had for their former company to themselves. "Be loyal to yourself," was the common theme.

Dissemination

In addition to the actual book, I have been able to disseminate the findings of my research through a variety of methods. I have written several articles which have been published on my own and other blogs. To date, I have been interviewed for six podcasts with human resource and career professionals, including being a guest on Career Talk, Sirius XM channel 132. I facilitated a panel on Career Game Changers for a women's retreat and will present at a state human resources association later this summer.

Reflection

Although the book is not a commercial success, its message is resonating with those who have read it. It is rewarding to help others prepare for the age of job uncertainty.

I know this undertaking would not have been possible without my DM education. It was natural for me to network and reach out to academic resources from different disciplines as I had learned to do in the DM program. Many of my professors are acknowledged in the book's Dedication.

It is my hope to be able to contribute to future DM students' educational journey. Perhaps one day this work might even be used to teach qualitative research interviews and provide an example of practitioner-scholar research in the DM program.

Keywords
Fired, Job Loss, Layoffs, Qualitative Interviews, Career, Management, Employee Engagement

About the Author: Nancy Koury King, DM
Dr. King has been a health care executive for over 25 years. Currently she serves as the president of Westminster Canterbury at Home, a home health and hospice agency in Virginia Beach and president of Senior Options, a national home health and hospice advisory firm. A Mandel Nonprofit Fellow and a Mitchell Morse Scholarship recipient, Dr. King earned her Doctor of Management degree from the Weatherhead School of Management, Case Western Reserve University in 2004. Her dissertation was on the social capital of nonprofit leaders with Melvin Smith, PhD, serving as her dissertation advisor. Dr. King is the author of "Fired: How to manage your career in the age of job uncertainty."

Jonathan Brewster

The Doctor of Management (DM) at Case Western Reserve University (CWRU) program taught me how to identify and articulate a problem, research that problem, and apply the research findings (based upon a scientific approach) to real-world solutions.

Mergers are Won on the Floorplates, Not Just the Boardroom

In October 2015, I left a major biomedical company, Company X, after a successful career in sales and sales management. In 2015, Company X acquired a competitor, Company Y. At that time, I elected to take a voluntary severance. Not long after I left, I began to receive calls from several of my former co-workers that the integration of the two companies was not going well. I had heard repeatedly that most mergers fail to realize the objectives that were expected. I listened to my former colleagues with curiosity, wondering if this merger would fit that conventional wisdom. People in the post-merger organization seemed confused, resistant, and generally frustrated about their work life, primarily as they spoke about a changing corporate culture (Buono, Bowditch, & Lewis, 1985). I often heard, "I do not know where I fit in anymore."

At this point, I was not planning to return to the new Company Z (XY), in any capacity. As I listened to the people that contacted me, I began to realize that it might be worthwhile to familiarize myself with some of the research around corporate culture and organizational integration. I delved into the research because I was fascinated by the problems my friends and colleagues were facing. In order to understand those problems, I needed a framework. I was not looking for wisdom that is more conventional or common sense, but rather a rigorous framework with which to understand the situation.

The Doctor of Management (DM) at Case Western Reserve University (CWRU) program taught me how to identify and articulate a problem, research that problem, and apply the research findings (based upon a scientific approach) to real-world solutions. In my case, I began to do an extensive literature search, starting with the broad category of post-merger integration. After reading a diverse collection of academic papers, as well as some of the classic research in the area of post-merger integration, it became apparent that this integration was failing. As I read more and more research in this broad area, the issues of corporate culture and integration resonated with me regarding the new organization. The research pointed to intentionality, that the post-merger integration had to be directed and lead in a very intentional manner. In fact, this merger was in jeopardy of failing because of a lack of intentionally managing the integration process (Stahl & Voigt, 2008).

> One of the greatest benefits of the DM program was that I was taught to think critically and more analytically based upon evidence, not just 'common sense'.

I found the framework I was looking for in several papers (Birkinshaw, Bresman, & Håkanson, 2000; Stahl & Voigt, 2008). That framework was the duality and interdependence of human and task integration. Human integration is defined as the creation of positive attitudes toward the integration among all employees (Birkinshaw et al., 2000), as well as developing a shared identity (Stahl & Voigt, 2008). Task integration was defined as all the activities that lead to operational synergies (Birkinshaw et al., 2000), as well as the transfer of capabilities and resource sharing, and consolidation (Stahl & Voigt, 2008).

I shared my findings with my former colleagues on subsequent calls. The predictable became apparent, as I was asked to come back and join the local office. My new role was not in sales and sales management but now in operations. My objective was to stabilize the organization. I had familiarized myself with the research in this area of post-merger integration and corporate culture. Having found a framework in which to analyze the issues, I accepted the position and returned. It was just one year after taking the voluntary severance.

Two of the three local offices of which I was responsible were now comprised of a mix of X and Y employees, all having the symptoms of a troubled integration. People congregated in workstations as members of the original organizations. There were the 'X' people and the 'Y' people. Most were not clear to whom they reported, customers' deliveries were suffering, and decisions seemed slow in the making. The environment was as bad, if not worse, than I expected. No one was happy.

Human Integration
Human integration essentially covers creating a new culture, not X or Y, but a Z made up of the values and norms of X and Y. This human integration is a long process, involving communication, shared experiences, and common goals (Birkinshaw et al., 2000). A few examples will illustrate this.

Birkinshaw et al. (2000) wrote about the need for rapid communication about a merger, convening meetings to answer questions and allay fears, quick decisions, and cross-team meetings. Upon returning, I immediately met personally with everyone I could. These meetings were often very short, but I felt it was important to make myself available and answer any questions (Birkinshaw et al., 2000). These meetings were also important because, as Birkinshaw et al. (2000) states, leaders in the integration process must be visible.

These meetings were productive because I quickly realized that people required clarity of their roles and the organizational structure. I created a traditional hierarchical organization and organizational chart that was easily understood. It also provided clear lines of reporting. In fact, when I presented this to one of the operations managers after meeting with him, his response was, "I have been waiting for one of these for over a year. Now I know where I fit."

It also became apparent that I had to work on developing a common language. Every discipline has a specialized language, as every company does. This common language identifies and promotes in group and out group membership, as well as facilitates task accomplishment. Our common language was not a list of abbreviations, but rather a common web-based operating system. Both X and Y, pre-merger, used different web-based operating systems. The systems allowed orders to be placed and scheduled deliveries, as well as developed daily workflow requirements to complete and ship orders to customers. Essentially these web-based systems are the heart of the day-to-day functioning of the companies.

Company X and Company Y did not use the same system. The operating system that was adopted originated from Company X and the Company Y employees were resisting using this system. Unfortunately, adopting it was not an option. I heard the Y employees often lament that they were faster if they did 'it' the old Y way. Through meetings, patient instruction, aligning the department heads, and generally taking every opportunity to explain why, the system was broadly utilized.

About a year after I had returned, I was walking through the warehouse. I overheard one of the Y workers criticize another office, not because it was largely comprised of X workers, but because it was in another state, another geographical location. He referred to the people there, not as X employees, but as Y employees of that geographical location. I realized, for just a moment that the human integration through a common language was beginning to take hold.

Task Integration
Task integration is the transfer of capabilities and resource sharing (Stahl & Voigt, 2008). I began to develop the task integration along the lines of, "everyone doing the same thing the same way," despite there being an X way and a Y way for each specific task. Many tasks were common between the two companies: we were in the same industry and had to perform the same operational functions. As you can imagine, the lack of intentionally managing the processes created a great deal of confusion. As a result, customer service and deliveries suffered.

I quickly created small working groups specific to a task to determine the best way to define task processes. The groups not only met to achieve that objective, but also to mix X and Y employees. This began to create a shared social identity and trust among the group members, something Stahl addresses as so important to the integration (Stahl & Voigt, 2008). Birkinshaw et al. (2000) stated this, in that human integration facilitates task integration. Otherwise, both sides do not know each other and a high level of suspicion about motives ensues. The lack of trust becomes evident. The task integration, like the human integration, cannot be separated nor are they quickly accomplished (Birkinshaw et al., 2000).

If it is true that most mergers and acquisitions fail to realize the intended objectives, then they are lost in the integration at the floorplate level, the meeting room level, and the customer service employee level, not necessarily the boardroom. It is the local intentional integration activities, both human and task, that create a new successful company.

The result of applying the principles garnered from the literature and research was two-fold. First, this project gained high visibility as a bit of a success story. Company Z steadily ascended in the national operational ranking and stayed there. We continue to perform in the top 25%, improving as more issues are addressed.

Secondly, I began to be recognized as having some credibility in turning around an organization struggling with a post-merger integration. This was directly attributable to defining the multiple problems, reviewing organizational research literature (particularly post-merger integration), developing the applicable framework, and acting on that framework. Other opportunities have become available because of this work.

I often hear that management is just 'common sense'. It is, but management is also a science and science is supported by research. One of the greatest benefits of the DM program was that I was taught to think critically and more analytically based upon evidence, not just 'common sense'. Included in this was learning the skill to assimilate prior knowledge. A further skill was to take that knowledge and use it to manage, to implement change. I could not have successfully navigated this integration without the skills I learned in the program. Knowing how to identify and apply prior knowledge in solving real-world problems is the crux of the value of the D.M. program.

Keywords

Merger, Post-Merger Integration, Company Culture, Intentionality

About the Author: Jonathan Brewster, DM

Dr. Brewster has worked in the medical device industry, primarily in sales and sales management, and more recently in operations. Presently he is employed as a field operations manager, assisting field offices in improving structure and processes to support sales. Dr. Brewster holds an engineering degree from the United States Merchant Marine Academy, a Master's degree from Carnegie Mellon University, and is a graduate of the Doctor of Management program from Case Western Reserve University.

Mark Engle

Observing a problem but not being able to put my thumb on the cause was the driving force behind my decision to attend Case Western Reserve University (CWRU) and pursue a Doctor of Management (DM) degree with a concentration in nonprofit management. I wanted to help boards function at their full potential and I was hungry for the skills and knowledge to identify and solve these problems directly.

Building Better Boards Through Governance and Strategic Decision Making

The Case for Obtaining a DM

When I started working with several nonprofit association board of directors at Association Management Center (AMC), I could tell that they were doing just fine; they were running meetings efficiently, solving small issues before they became bigger problems, and acting cohesively. However, when I witnessed other boards at outside associations, I noticed something was wrong. It appeared that the boards made decisions that vastly reduced their effectiveness, yet I could never figure out why. The problem was that I was not even thinking in terms of conflict and decision quality. Observing a problem but not being able to put my thumb on the cause was the driving force behind my decision to attend Case Western Reserve University (CWRU) and pursue a Doctor of Management (DM) degree with a concentration in nonprofit management. I wanted to help boards function at their full potential and I was hungry for the skills and knowledge to identify and solve these problems directly.

I conducted research with Weatherhead School of Management's Human Resource Policy Professor Emeritus Dr. Paul Salipante and investigated seven high-performing boards. Being a DM student at CWRU helped me understand how to conduct vigorous investigative research in identifying and solving problems with board governance. The biggest "*aha!*" moment in my research was discovering the gaps in board decision-making processes, which usually are driven by affective or emotional arguments instead of cognitive arguments. However, high-performing boards manage the affective and cognitive conflict well enough to advance decision-making.

Having knowledge of such research and following my findings opened up a new line of inquiry about conflict and decision quality. I have been advancing this research since graduation and have been educating boards about proficient board composition and strategy, even advancing tools and techniques to use in the boardroom.

The Significance of a DM Education

Another way that the DM program and education influenced my life is in teaching me how to conduct and apply rigorous research, which affects my approach to working with my skilled team members and employees at AMC and with my clients. The first (and perhaps foremost) takeaway I have is that I must constantly seek new knowledge through research. This is why it is increasingly important, for me and for anyone in the professional world, to verify sources of information, especially in today's social media environment. When I am seeking information or trying to solve a problem, I examine my source and analyze if there are any inherent biases. I have learned to only seek vetted academic journals with rigorous editing and approval processes for verification. People tend to take any information on the Internet at face value. Unfortunately, we live in a day and age where "fake news" is a household term, and all news sources should, in theory, be credible. However, that is not always the case; even if you find a credible article on Facebook, for instance, it does not mean that all articles you find on Facebook will be credible.

Due to rigorous research and the sources of my own dissertation being questioned and speculated on, CWRU trained me to be cynical, such as in deconstructing an article and receiving a critical assessment of my own findings. Cynicism is incredibly important for the sake of veritable research and best practices, but it is not always the best approach to communicating with my client partners, with whom AMC takes pride in maintaining long-lasting partnerships. I am glad to have so much practice in ensuring accuracy because that mindset is an intentional worldview and work ethic that transcends academia and occupation. However, I try to dial back my outward cynicism when it comes to my clients. I am mindful of how I conduct conversations so that I am still authentically inquisitive without being negative or defensive, especially when asking questions. I help my clients identify the issues they are facing, even when they cannot articulate these issues. To be a good leader, I must ask questions and verify information, but I can do that and still be approachable, open, friendly, and diplomatic. In working with my clients and during board meetings, I examine my sources of information and analyze them for any inherent biases. Once I deem the information reliable, I can determine the best method of finding the problems of practice; once identified, I can help my clients properly articulate the problems and move forward with solving the issues at hand.

How the DM has advanced my Career

Getting my DM has opened more doors for me. Beyond how it has shaped my research, I have more credibility and scope of influence as a DM from a rigorous program at a prestigious university. Association Forum of Chicagoland knew that I was helping boards improve

their governance structure, and they wanted to formally recognize how my efforts complemented my compelling title and position, which played a role into being nominated for its Samuel Shapiro Award for Outstanding CEO. Having the DM degree was significant, even critical, to my acceptance to the BoardSource program, from which I became a Certified Governance Trainer in 2013. BoardSource has validated

Getting my DM has opened more doors for me. Beyond how it has shaped my research, I have more credibility and scope of influence as a DM from a rigorous program at a prestigious university.

and challenging grounding, therefore, they only accepted applicants who could meet their high standards. This certification has allowed me to access BoardSource's resources, which I cite and apply frequently. Even without the certifications and awards, my DM helps me earn the trust of doctors and executive professionals. This, in turn, helps me reach and find solutions for more board members.

Post-CWRU Research

After composing my dissertation, I continued my doctoral research with Professor Will Brown of the Bush School of Government and Public

Service at Texas A&M University. We have since collaborated on several projects: we have presented the webinars "Board Member Recruitment Selection in Associations" at the American Society of Association Executives (ASAE) Foundation and "Oversight: Release Control to Empower Success" for BoardSource; and the presentation "The Right Board Leaders Translate to High Performance" for ASAE.

I have collaborated with other AMC staff and association experts for my presentations: with Judy Millesen and David Renz, governance experts and authors, for our "Board Performance — Practice Meets Theory" presentation at Association Forum of Chicagoland and AMC; with Dave Bergeson for the presentation "A Collision in Governance: Rules, Expectations, and Structure" for ABLI-American Bar Association; with Christie Tarantino and Nancy Green for the presentation "From Practice to Profession"; for ASAE Fellows; with Mary Beth Benner for the presentation "Governance Essentials" for Association Forum of Chicagoland; with Mary Byers for 5 presentations of "Exceptional Boards" for ASAE; with Anne Cordes for the webinar "Linking Boards and Strategy" at the Nursing Organizations Alliance; and facilitated with Jared D. Harris for the presentation "Effective Governance; Understanding Strategy and Values" at the Executive Leadership Program at the ASAE Annual Conference.

The topic of my research today has not strayed from my research at CWRU; rather, I have simply broadened the scope of my investigations in best practices for board governance and association management, all under the same domain in which it had always been. I have found that my dissertation was the first of many building blocks of effective board governance. One must start with the role of the board then the role of the staff within the board. Questions begin to arise: can one have a good board-staff partnership to drive performance? What do high-performing boards do? How do they accelerate decision-making? To find solutions to board questions and problems, one must start with the first building block. Consider the possible roots of the problem a board may face: is there a breakdown of trust? Is the problem a matter of board structure and process? Alternatively, is it simply the personalities of the board members? Those very different problems require very different approaches to find a solution.

One big problem I found is a learning gap in many associations and organizations between the staff and the boards. In these instances, the best governance practices are not taught to staff; rather, there is a trend of board members learning on the job, without proper training. That is why I am dedicated to building better boards from the ground up and continuing to support them so that they can optimize their board performance and function at a higher level. The objectives of my presentations and workshops have been to explore the roles and responsibilities of board members and give interactive learning activities with the presentation. Just because the board members often have to learn on the job, it does not mean that they cannot practice what they should do in a controlled setting.

Recently, I have been dedicating more time and research to investigating board problems even further upstream: the board selection processes. With AMC's clients and within the association community, I have observed that competent board populace precedes effective board governance and decision-making. The first building block is not simply the roles of the board members; it is the board members themselves and their own professional and interpersonal competencies. I have found it disturbing that unprofessional behavior and a lack of civility has crept into some boardrooms. While interpersonal relationships are not the cornerstone of association board performance, they can inhibit the boards overall collaboration and success. Having the foresight to see that any negative interpersonal relationships that can be prevented, such as a lack of general trust, I can identify ways to maintain this sense of trust and help the boards move forward in their strategies and capabilities. Sometimes, the decision of not just what topics come into the boardroom, but also who comes into the boardroom, makes a significant difference to board competency and quality. At Association Forum, I conduct a workshop, "Governance Essentials," that is paired with a book of the same name that AMC staff and I compiled, which dives deep into the process and results of good board selection.

I have sat in on more than 300 board meetings, but for the past three years, I have been particularly attentive in easing new board members' transition into their new roles and educating them on their new responsibilities. I like a very hands-on approach. I feel like a coach to association CEOs and board chairs. While I am helping board members figure out their own role in the board, I can also observe how they spend time together and see if there are any impediments to advancing strategy, enabling me to provide customized, real solutions to problems that I see and experience with the boards. Since there is always a role changeover in board member composition, new issues always arise. In this way, you can say that my work is never done, but it is exciting to constantly learn about new potential board issues, which broaden the scope of my continued research.

Post-CWRU Enterprises and Successes

Since graduating with my DM from CWRU, I have given many governance and leadership presentations, including at least five webinars, one web interview, and 19 onsite presentations. I have also facilitated four presentations, served on two panels, and returned to CWRU to present on "Group Conflict and Decision Making" at the Weatherhead School of Management's Transformative Leadership Symposium. I have also written seven articles for various journals on nonprofit governance.

The association companies where I usually give my presentations have demonstrated thought and career leadership in the association management industry and among professionals therein; they are where members, executives, and experts come together to share knowledge and gain more insights and education from each other. These centers include Association Forum, ASAE, and the Association Management Company Institute (AMCi). Most of the members are association CEOs, board chairs, chair elects, and other senior staff. We spend 75%–80% of our time together at forums sharing information such as our research findings, how we apply them, and other endeavors in the research pipeline. I am honored to present for so many C-suite professionals, earn their trust through my demonstrated competency as a DM, and help them recruit optimal board members to have effective board governance.

The Children's Arthritis and Rheumatology Research Alliance is a concrete example of the applications of my workshops and board auditing. They invited me to come speak about board development and asked me to audit and critique their board meeting. They liked my lecture topics and how I teach and they wanted to put it into practice themselves. They have consistently invited me back to be a critical lens and help them identify where they missed opportunities to make further advances because of issues in the boardroom. This has been repeated across a variety of organizations that want to operate more efficiently and keep inviting me back for more audits, critiques, and recommendations.

Case Study: Group O
One case in particular that stands out is the governance consulting work that Dr. Brown and I conducted with a healthcare association, which shall remain anonymous and is referred to as Group O in a book for ASAE, *Recruit the Right Board: Proven Processes for Selecting Critical Competencies*, which was published in August 2019. Group O is a healthcare association that has more than 40,000 members and an annual revenue of more than $27 million. Like myself before I graduated with my DM from CWRU, they knew they needed help, but they could not quite figure out the exact source of their problems nor how to solve them. With such a populous membership, it was important that their board run efficiently and it did not. What they did know was that they wanted to create more transparency in the board's nomination, recruitment, and selection practices, because they needed additional skills and competencies to advance their strategic plan.

The board is composed of 11 members — who serve three-year terms — and four officers. The association had recently gone through multiple changes, not to mention a merger that consolidated the two original boards. Working with them, I recognized that they needed the most help with their selection process. Due to the recent merger, there was no clear, common, stated process of populating the board thereafter. Upon becoming stable, the board recognized that changes were necessary within the board's composition and structure to meet the association's needs, and this meant diversifying the skills and competencies of the board members.

We used three strategies to improve the transparency of the governance structure. We worked on strengthening and aligning the relationship between the staff and the boards, which improved transparency between them. With better collaboration between the two parties, the board formalized a publishing process for novice board member elections, thereby increasing the transparency of the board selection process. The selection process formalization involved turning Group

O's nominating committee into a leadership committee, which cultivates leaders by educating members on how to get involved in leadership opportunities at Group O and identifies a list of competencies to consider for all board candidates. After formalizing the board selection process, creating the leadership committee, and providing transparency in ideal leadership capabilities, the amount of applications increased from two or three to about 150.

What started as an education program and helping them reconstruct their board composition turned into a five-year relationship with Group O and continual workshops with them around board assessment, development, and orientation. The quality of competence at the table has vastly improved. Their latest round of directors is outstanding: they spend more time on strategy, and their capacity to make wise, consequential decisions is higher than ever before.

Keywords
Nonprofit Governance, Association Management, Board Governance

About the Author: Mark Engle, DM
Dr. Engle is an AMC principal and frequent author and speaker on governance and high-performing organizations. He is a faculty member of ASAE's Exceptional Boards program and a Fellow at ASAE and the Mandel Center for Nonprofit Leadership. He formerly served as a chief staff executive for trade associations and professional societies for 29 years. Dr. Engle has participated in more than 300 board meetings during his career and serves on six boards of directors.

Noble C. Philip

The CWRU education provided me a means of engaging the world of the inner-city communities, the poor without a voice, allowing me to blend my three different worlds: a successful business career, exposure to academia, and the grittiness of a hardscrabble life in the inner-city.

Understanding Backwards, Living Forward

In April 2013, on a post-retirement flight back from Europe, I learned of the Weatherhead School of Management Doctor of Management (DM) Program. It was tucked away in the Economist magazine that I stowed to read. I had taken early retirement in March 2013, because I was troubled about the decay, caused by burgeoning crime that was taking root in the capital city, in the country of my birth. I had a compulsion to help, but no defined route. In 2019, I appreciate better that I am wrestling with a 'wicked' problem about how a nation can reverse the grip of crime that devastates its youth. While I had limited ways to approach this previously, now I have the tools to abstract the issues and to tackle them in a systematic manner. This is the essence of the transformation that took place between 2013 and 2016: the new capacity to derive abstract understandings from the world of academia and use these insights to seek a way of advancing a better way forward.

This is what the doctoral program at Case Western Reserve University (CWRU) has done for me. I did not, at the time of my entry to CWRU, know that academia could speak to the issues about inducing change at the community level that bothered me. Being a business leader gives power to take your organization along a specific path. It is a closed system, with a fairly clear penalty and reward system. Working at a community level, the dynamics are different in that you are only one player in a milieu where many interests intersect. There is an imprecise definition of root causes as it is easier for most people to respond to the effects that are seen. To have the resources aligned to the need is not done by one's fiat but it has to be negotiated. CWRU's courses in collective action and managing complex systems proved to be invaluable in the context of managing change at the community level. The context provided toward understanding the economic and global issues is invaluable, but this realisation only grows post-graduation as one struggles to explain how the larger structural issues impact a nation and a community. The notion of ethical behavior and doing good grounds the actions that one takes and creates a filter through which the actions of others can be understood.

The CWRU education provided me a means of engaging the world of the inner-city communities, the poor without a voice, allowing me to blend my three different worlds: a successful business career, exposure to academia, and the grittiness of a hardscrabble life in the inner-city. My world prior to 2013 was largely lived in boardrooms and through the presentation of plans to advance consumer brands. If one measures success by growth in profitability, I could be said to be successful in that the businesses I lead for more than 30 years broadened and consolidated their franchises to become the leaders in their spheres. But this success was not satisfying since many citizens were left off the escalator of growth because of the nature of the neo-liberal capitalism model. The income and social inequality gap became stark and crime rose in a response to the exclusion of the poor in the society. But this is all shrouded in opaqueness since the narrative is focused on the behavior of the poor and not on what causes them to behave in the particular manner. The tools gained at CWRU allowed for the unmasking of the agendas behind the narratives. They have sharpened my ability to communicate with a national audience the truths about life in the hard places we call the inner-city. I have understood that most people in my nation have no sense of how difficult and brutish life is for those who live in the inner-city. The steepness of the slope — be it basic health,

> The multi-disciplinary nature of the CWRU doctoral program has equipped me to speak about this work in the communities from various angles, opening up the dialogue with a wide range of interested parties.

schooling, or garbage removal issues — those residents must climb is not appreciated. I consider myself uniquely placed because my business career provides the entrance into the places of power, the rigor of my academic journey provides the analytical tools to dissect the issues and the ability to live among the poor and to have a seat at their table provides the language and the experiences that need to be used to raise national awareness.

Trinidad and Tobago, my homeland, has long been the jewel of the Caribbean. Its importance stems from the use of the energy resources in the creation of heavy industry. One of the resident companies here is the largest supplier of methanol to North America and a significant player in Europe. The country is among the top producers in BP's operations worldwide. Yet, the poverty rate remains stubbornly at 21%. Despite rapid improvements in the country's infrastructure, the conditions of the schools and the main hospitals do not measure up to the needs of the population. The wealth has not trickled down. The quality of life in the urban centre has deteriorated even as serious crime has escalated while unintended consequences are influencing other parts of the country.

Kurt Lewin is quoted as saying, "If you want to truly understand something, try to change it". I can affirm the truth of this. One of the main findings of my dissertation was the importance of preserving access to public spaces in these communities. The importance of the community groups was underlined especially when communal resources were put under strain. For those interested in community change, the key lesson is the recursive nature of change. Even if one is able to abstract and simplify the relationships that inform what happens in the communities, there is the need to think about change in a modular fashion.

Since graduation, I have been working on improving the capacity of a community group in an attempt to bolster their impact on their immediate community. I have chosen to work with the young men in the under 25 years of age cohort, which is the one most at risk of being co-opted by gangs or who, in some other fashion, may be induced to live an aimless life. These young men are at a crucial turning point in their lives – they have finished high school and can proceed to university or they can sink into mediocrity and empty lives. My goal is to have them make proper life decisions as a foundation for their own long-term well-being. In doing this, I realized that to boost the potential for success required the cooperation of the family; but this is a place of uneven cooperation because their parents themselves do not have the experience to guide the child into higher education. Even when the cooperation was forthcoming, there was a challenge from peer influences, expressed through the adoption of urban style dress, which is antithetical to integration into university life or work life. The importance of the elders in the community and their influence in ensuring that no single community group dominates while still preserving communal pride, a major finding of my dissertation, has been underlined. The problem that emerged was how to nudge these elders into keeping the young not only involved but committed to the goals of the broader community. It appears that the elders believe that whatever activities worked in the past and the way those were operationalized is still the path to tread. To get them to acknowledge that the young men have different life experiences and expectations is a tremendous difficulty that requires complex negotiations.

Change in communities is bi-directional. The community life impacts the family and the individuals but the same is true in the reverse. My dissertation's model required modification in that it omitted the issue of personal credibility, which is won slower than molasses in January. Community leaders do not automatically wish for and are not supportive of the change for better since they can be invested in the status quo. The family can be content once the young man does not get arrested by the police. The average young man cannot see beyond the next week in terms of planning and makes no connection between personal habits and his success. The community engages in a discourse of deficit and suffers from a 'poverty of imagination' — the inability to see a future that is different from their present circumstances. The key to unlocking this conundrum now appears to be personal credibility, which was not included in my original model. After three years, progress has been painfully slow but there has been success in that one young man returned to university and completed his program and three others are entering a university program. Unfortunately, others are still listlessly going through life below their potential.

One of the key benefits of the doctoral program has been the understanding of the importance of dissemination. This ability to build a communication network at both the informal and formal levels is a critical asset in creating change in the communities. The need to be clear about the voice to be adopted has been a powerful lesson learned as I seek to provide greater clarity about the needs and life experiences in the communities at risk. The multi-disciplinary nature of the CWRU doctoral program has equipped me to speak about this work in the communities from various angles, opening up the dialogue with a wide range of interested parties.

As much as the business leaders espouse the need for intervention in these crime-prone areas and express concern about violent extremism, they are not minded to move beyond voicing platitudes. I have done research on public sentiment about the need for direct intervention in the lives of the poor and inner-city communities and have presented it to several business leaders, but this has not materialized the support of business groups in any tangible manner. On the other hand, the local US Embassy has taken note of the work being done, and together with the local media association, they have invited me to participate in creating possible solutions. My view is that this particular aspect of the journey will happen slowly, but the invitations continue to come in and I will continue to speak at every opportunity.

I have been using the mainstream media and an online media vehicle as the conduits for my engagement with the national public. I have a weekly column in the online media outlet and am a frequent contributor in the leading mainstream newspaper. I am able to use these outlets as a means of highlighting and explaining life in the communities, where I work. The CWRU program has taught me two important principles: be rigorous in reaching conclusions and be aware of how the issues are framed. A major asset, as a CWRU graduate, is the continued access to the library, which has enabled me to do the requisite ongoing research in support of my writing. Through the feedback mechanisms employed by both outlets, I am able to understand how my writings are received and therefore am better able to articulate the issues. The writings have opened doors for me to discuss broader national matters at several levels, from the business leaders, to influencers to the community organizers. Because of the library access support, I have not had to retract any of my contributions because of public challenges even though I have been able to learn from the discussions how I may better articulate my position.

Van De Ven (2011) captures my post-graduation experience, "connecting theory and practice is no simple trick; but when it occurs it can trigger dazzling insights" (p. 260). As an immersed change agent, I am beginning to examine other plausible alternative models for the dealing with the research problem I confronted in my dissertation: why do some communities do well, and others do not. I seek to be situationally relevant and I am interpreting the data collected through my interactions with the players in the community in that specific context.

I am engaged in an experiment in which I am observing the growth of fifteen boys in a single cohort to discover how they may choose the path to be productive citizens. Their behavior and those of their family and community elders form the platform for triggering their decisions. On the other hand, I am engaging with the national community to buy space for these boys and others like them to explore a better life opportunity. The effort is to create purveyors of hope rather than continue the dialogue of despair. But to achieve that change, which is a bi- or multi-directional activity, requires interaction with many players and the change is not linear. Wicked problems are truly unique and have no definitive path but as my experience shows, the path evolves.

My continuing research could benefit from the integration of broad economic thinking as applied to the circumstances of these communities. My dissertation could have been greatly enhanced by the inclusion of economic thinking. I believe that the work of Karl Polyani and the political economic theorists and the work of development economists in the Latin American region — like Andre Gunder Frank, a Latin American economist, and George Beckford, a Caribbean economist — would have added more context to the development of my initial model and may have provided other possible outcomes. To this end, I have begun reading their work and thinking about how these may be integrated into the work being done as well as the theoretical framework that is possible. It is my view that this strand of research may help to better explain the underlying reasons why the institutions may or may not perform as expected or as desired. In the original research, institutions (such as the police, schools, and health facilities) underperformed and this tipped communities into despair.

The experience at CWRU has changed my life and is helping to change the lives of those who live in the communities in which I work. In this, John Locke, the English Philosopher, was right: improvement of knowledge helps both the learner and those with whom he comes into contact.

Keywords
Social Inequity, Institutional Resources, Discourse Deficit, Community

About the Author: Noble C. Philip, DM
Dr. Philip is a retired business executive, living in Trinidad and Tobago. He is passionate about his home country and desires to help make it a better place. Dr. Philip's work post-retirement has been focused on the youth, both at the community level in the inner-city and new entrants into the business world. His world has been enriched by his exposure to academic literature.

Andreas Jurt

The DM program is unique in the way it stimulates you to think about organizations and markets from a design perspective which enables managers to logically structure their thinking in an interdisciplinary way and to deconstruct complexity.

Qualitative Research and Applying Blue Ocean Strategy

Business Setting and Problem of Practice

I have 25 years of business experience as a banker revising and judging multiple business plans written by small and mid-sized companies (SME) in Switzerland. These companies were applying for bank credit, either to boost their working capital or to foster new investments in order to grow. Now, as a consultant, I had to write one of these business plans, from scratch, for a Swiss company looking to expand into new territories.

In the last year, I worked as a consultant at AJ-Business Impact PLUS. One of my clients is a privately held enterprise that has been around for more than 200 years and is recognized as a premium brand in the tool making industry for watches and jewelry. Ninety-eight percent of its sales are located in those industries and the rest is allocated to micromechanics. Dependent to the high cyclical business trends, the CEO has decided to explore the opportunity to leverage their technical knowledge in order to penetrate other industries such as aerospace, defense and robotics for the sake of diversification and new sales.

At the end of 2017, the company had annual sales of around USD 16 million (40% in Switzerland and 60% in other countries around the world) with a range of more than 12,000 products and it employed around 70 people. However, bottom-line (EBITDA) and the top-line growth (sales) were too weak to generate sufficient cash for new strategic investments. Indeed, a real problem of practice!

How to Tackle that Problem?

Bankers, investors, and clients have to believe that a proposed business story is possible, credible, and profitable in a reasonable time (four to six years is a standard pay-back period). In order to attract bankers and new private investors (purely private equity or long term oriented strategic individuals), I conceptualized a new business plan for 2019–2023 based on my Doctor of Management (DM) Program learnings: 1) Define clearly a well stated problem of practice; 2) Inquire if this problem is a real problem; 3) Formulate hypotheses; 4) Conduct a qualitative research based on grounded theory; 5) Check the validity of the findings; 6) Proceed to a scenario analysis based on probabilities; and 7) Implementation.

The former business plan was written by left-brain engineering managers who advocated about their high-end products and its historic legitimacy in its key market without a deep sense of marketing. It was a technical and single market approach.

Inspired by Blue Ocean Strategy (Kim & Mauborgne, 2004), I designed a theoretical conceptual framework on focusing how and to what extent the company already had some of the key organizational capabilities (e.g., machines and human capital) to penetrate into new territories such as aerospace and defense. Blue Ocean Strategy is the simultaneous pursuit of differentiation to open up a new market space and create new demand. It is about creating and capturing uncontested market space, thereby making the competition irrelevant.

I interviewed 10 CEOs and 15 procurement managers in new industries in order to gain inside knowledge for a better understanding of the underlying needs and requirements, such as certifications, of the new markets (i.e., products, services, operational efficiency, and prize sensitivity). I designed a semi-structured questionnaire and used selective probing to better see 'the forest and not only the trees.' The emerging key findings (e.g., Swiss-made, company history, market recognition to manufacture precise, safe small tools, same meaning and language of engineering focus, and operational efficiency) showed me that we should focus, first, on the aerospace sector where we could materialize rapidly new business.

Backed-up by quantitative papers about the market potential worldwide for tools I got the confirmation that the aerospace and defense sectors were the industries in which we could rapidly collect the "low hanging fruits," in terms of immediate sales, without investing unnecessary money in "CapEx" that defines the need to undertake new projects or investments by the firm. Why? It is a question of focus, opportunity cost, engineering, operational capabilities, and what I call the "learning curve" in order to deliver rapid results.

Now, we had to position the company in order to be appealing and attractive for future clients and lenders. What is the company's unique selling proposition in term of differentiating factors compared to competitors if the company wants to implement successfully the Blue Ocean Strategy?

Relying on the company's embedded values and its market recognition, I positioned it as a Flourishing Enterprise whose vision is 'doing good is not good enough, doing well is better'. The business plan explained in a credible and reliable manner how the company embraces embedded sustainability without neglecting profitable growth by caring equally about the well-being of its stakeholders. I enhanced their concept by the dimension of mindfulness in the sense to see the world with its risks and opportunities as it is now and without mind wandering how nice it was in the past.

What does the company stand for? My business plan was conceptually designed in order to position the company in the market as a producer who makes Swiss-made *premium brand* products instead of buying them from other suppliers. To deliver our promise, we have the best people to be fast and cost efficient in terms of operational excellence and to be recognized ultimately as client excellence. No company can be everything all at once. We market our company as *product excellence*; first with a focus on value pricing (margin sensitive) and a cost management inspired by an approach of marginal costs versus marginal benefits (volume approach to increase the rotation of its inventory).

Results

The company's ambition is to achieve sales of USD 20 million by 2023, where USD 5 million will be realized by the new sectors. After 10 months in 2019, we are 6 % YTD above budget, and we have gained some positive momentum in the aerospace sector. Some key actors of this industry know us better and they are doing their due diligence to measure where the company may best fit their products needs. Together we are evaluating common business opportunities for tools and consumables. The Swiss Army will buy new air fighters. Five companies are competing (3 European, 2 American). Also, due to my international experience and the DM program at Case Western Reserve University (CWRU), I have more credibility when I speak to each CEO bargaining for new clients and the banks did like my original and new minded business plan. They understand and support our vision, mission, and action plan "to increase the size of the pie."

Conclusion

I would like to highlight why the DM program was valuable for me. It allowed me to become a better decision maker, an investor, and a consultant. The real added values or the cutting-edge advantage are the design aspect and the focus on interdisciplinary thinking. Looking at and analyzing a real problem of practice from all angles (e.g., economic, managerial, sociological, linguistic) helps to understand and screen it with pragmatism, efficiency, and effectiveness. The DM program is unique in the way it stimulates you to think about organizations and markets from a design perspective which enables managers to logically structure their thinking in an interdisciplinary way and to deconstruct complexity.

For me, the DM Program at Case Western Reserve University reunites "the magic triangle." It is a challenging program, it has exceptional academic and professional experiences of the professors, and it has avid students coming from all fields and all regions in the world, empowered by a demonstrated track record of successful leadership and who are inspired to keep on learning and ready to share their knowledge.

Keywords

Blue Ocean Strategy, Flourishing Enterprise, Qualitative Research

About the Author: Andreas Jurt, DM

Dr. Jurt has worked as an independent consultant for small and midsized companies in Switzerland and abroad since 2018. His specializations are strategy design and business development in new markets. Prior to this work, he was a banker (Managing Director) for more than 25 years with focus on Wealth Management and Corporate Finance. Dr. Jurt's educational background includes a Doctor of Management (DM 2015, Case Western Reserve University) and Executive MBA (EMBA 2007, Bern-Rochester).

"*Innovation comes out of great human ingenuity and very personal passions.*"

Megan Smith

Innovator

Connecting new radical ideas drawing on heterogeneous knowledge and novel ideas emerging from doctor of management study

Michael W. Grieves

The first semester in 1997 of EDM program was essentially about learning to think differently. For those of us that had spent our adult lives in the business world, understanding the academic approach, methodologies, and even culture was a significant change in mindset. It was a plunge into unfamiliar waters of new concepts, new literature sources, new methodologies, and new ways of thinking about things.

Digital Twin: Developing a 21st Century Product Model

Introduction

I have always had a fascination with information. I was fortunate enough to put that fascination into practice at an early age. In the 60s as a junior in high school, I was selected for a National Science Foundation program at Oakland University in Rochester, Michigan, for a program called "Math Camp". While the math part was interesting, the real allure of the camp was learning to program in FORTRAN using the University's IBM 1620 mainframe.

By my first year in college, I was working as a mainframe systems programmer on timesharing operating systems. In my early 20s, I was involved in both an executive and technical capacity, with some of the most advanced computer systems in existence, such as the Illiac IV. By my 30s, I had started my own computer company and worked with some of the pioneers of the information networking area, such as Dr. Robert Metcalf, inventor of Ethernet.

By 1997, I entered the Doctor of Management (DM) program at Case Western Reserve University (CWRU) and was interested in moving beyond the practical aspects of information processing and delving deeper into the underlying theory and constructs about information itself.

I was particularly interested in the idea that information that was embedded in physical objects could be stripped from those objects and created as an entity in its own right. Because of the exponential increases in computing capability, as predicted by Moore's Law, we were rapidly approaching a point where the information that we could obtain by being in physical possession of a physical object could be replicated digitally within a computer. This idea of the duality of a physical object and its embedded information in a virtual/digital object was a concept that begin to crystallize early on in the DM program.

This duality of objects, both physical and virtual, today is known as the Digital Twin. While this concept was ahead of its time at the beginning of this millennium because of its compute intensive requirements, the exponential increases in both hardware and software made the Digital Twin a reality by the middle of the current decade.

The Digital Twin
The Digital Twin is one of the top concepts in product realization. Gartner, a leading technology research firm, has included the Digital Twin in their "Top Ten Strategic Technology Trends" for the past three years. However, an Internet search five years ago on the term "Digital Twin" may have produced only a handful of hits. Today, that same search produces over a million entries. A search of "Digital Twin" images produces a half a million pictures of products. These products include airplanes, ships, oil rigs, power turbines, and medical devices to name a few.

A product is basically defined as a man-made object that performs a function or functions for a user (Grieves, 2011). Products are tangible as they are atom based. Products run the spectrum, being as simple and small as paper clips and being as large and complex as aircraft carriers and spacecrafts. Products not only consist of material, but also contain information. That information is embedded within the product itself by virtue of its atomic and molecular make up. Information such as its dimensions, structural characteristics, weight, color, and everything else is dictated and embedded in a product by virtue of its material make up.

The Digital Twin is a conceptual model, which asserts that this embedded product information can exist digitally, independent of the physical product. This means that all products are dual in nature: products exist physically and virtually. At its optimum, any information that could be obtained from inspecting a physical manufactured product can be obtained from its Digital Twin.

The Digital Twin model is shown in Figure 1. The Digital Twin consists of three distinct elements. On the left side is the physical product that has always existed. It can also be thought of as the Physical Twin (Grieves, 2019). On the right side is its virtual counterpart or what has come to be known as the Digital Twin. The third element is the connection between the physical and virtual versions. Data from the physical world is collected and transmitted to its Digital Twin. The information from the digital version can be transmitted and used in the physical world.

Digital Twin
Physical and Virtual Products

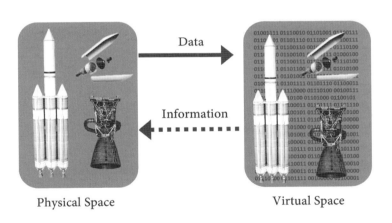

Physical Space　　　　　　　　Virtual Space

Figure 1

The Digital Twin model was first publicly introduced in 2002 as a concept for Product Lifecycle Management (PLM) without giving the model a name (Grieves 2002). As shown in Figure 2, that model had a fourth element, Virtual Subspaces (VS1,VS2,VSn). This indicated that while only one physical space exists, multiple virtual spaces can and do exist. A physical car can be crash tested once. A virtual car can be crash tested over and over. This element was dropped to simplify the model. The model was originally named the Mirrored Spaces Model (MSM) (Grieves, 2005), but later changed to the Information Mirroring Model (Grieves,

Conceptual Ideal for PLM

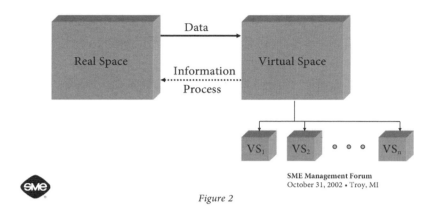

Figure 2

2006). The model was finally referred to as the Digital Twin (Grieves, 2011), a name that John Vickers of NASA had coined for the model.

There will be different types of Digital Twins, depending on the phase of the product's lifecycle (Grieves & Vickers 2016). I have defined three types of Digital Twins: the Digital Twin Prototype (DTP), the Digital Twin Instance (DTI), and the Digital Twin Aggregate (DTA).

The DTP describes the prototypical physical product and all its variants. It contains the informational sets necessary to describe and produce a physical version that duplicates or twins the virtual version. These informational sets include, but are not limited to, product requirements, fully annotated 3D model, Bill of Materials (with material specifications), behavior simulations, Bill of Processes, Bill of Services, and Bill of Disposal. This Digital Twin exists before the physical version and takes shape over time. As I often say, "No one goes into a factory, randomly pounds on some metal, and hopes an airplane comes out."

The DTI describes a specific corresponding physical product that an individual Digital Twin remains linked to throughout the life of that individual physical product. The DTI captures the specifics of manufacturing the product, the "As Built". It then contains the information on how that product is maintained and used throughout its life. DTIs exist only for products where it is important to have information about that product throughout its life. Airplanes, rockets, high-end manufacturing equipment, and even automobiles have or will have DTIs. Paper clips will not.

DTAs are the aggregation or composite of all the DTIs. DTAs are both longitudinal and latitudinal representations of behavior. Their longitudinal value is to correlate previous state changes with subsequent behavioral outcome. This enables, for example, prediction of component failure when certain sensor data occurs. Latitudinal value can occur via a learning process, when a small group of DTIs learn from actions. That learning can be conveyed to subsequent DTIs. Figure 3 shows an example of DTI and DTA use in interrogation, prediction, and learning.

Interrogative/Predictive/Learning

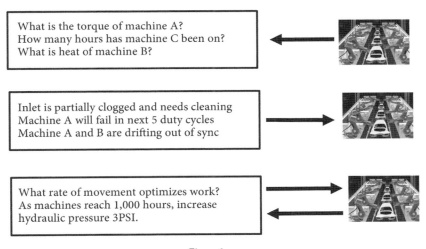

Figure 3

The value of the Digital Twin is that information is a substitute for wasted physical resources. Bits are cheaper than atoms, with bits getting cheaper at an exponential rate and atoms getting more expensive at the rate of inflation. We can use the information of Digital Twins to create, produce, operate, and support products more effectively and efficiently. The Digital Twin model as shown in Figure 2 seems to imply that the Digital Twin and Physical Twin reside in two distinct spaces, Physical and Digital space. We work in one space at a time in a single mode fashion and then transfer data and information to the other space.

That, in practice, is how we have worked with the Digital Twin model. We worked in virtual space and translated that information into physical space to create actual products. We manufactured those products in physical space and sent that data about the actual product to virtual space to create a DTI of the physical product.

This single mode of working with Digital Twins is evolving into a mixed-mode of working with the advancements in Augmented Reality (AR) technology. We are now able to overlay physical space with virtual space to work in both spaces simultaneously. For example, a technician can look at a turbine with AR and see blade speed, fuel flow, and heat maps.

The Digital Twin model has been used by NASA for spacecraft (Caruso et al., 2010, Glaessgen & Stargel 2012; Piascik et al., 2010) and by the U.S. Air Force for jet fighters (Tuegel, 2012), and is proposed for aircraft health in general (Warwick, 2014).

The Digital Twin has been proposed for robust deployment of Internet of Things (IoT) (Maher, 2018) and for factory production (Post et al., 2017). The oil industry is exploring the use of Digital Twin for ocean-based production platforms (Renzi et al., 2017). General Electric has used the term extensively, especially for power generation equipment (Economist, 2015), (Castellanos, 2017).

Digital Twins of smart homes have been proposed (Gopinath, 2019). The European Union is funding a major initiative on smart buildings that uses my concept and definitions (www.sphere.eu).

The Digital Twin and its Genesis in the DM Program

I will contend that it is rare where ideas pop out fully formed in a "Eureka!" moment; at least it is for me. Instead, I would liken it to being in a darkened room, where gradual lightening shows where all the furniture is placed. One first sees the dim outlines that as the illumination exposes richer and richer detail. My development of the Digital Twin concept followed that analogy.

My first semester in 1997 of DM program was essentially about learning to think differently. For those of us that had spent our adult lives in the business world, understanding the academic approach, methodologies, and even culture was a significant change in mindset. It was a plunge into unfamiliar waters of new concepts, new literature sources, new methodologies, and new ways of thinking about things.

What was serendipitous and beneficial for me were the 1998 semesters, spring and fall. Three courses in particular honed in on areas that were critically relevant to my interest in information. Specifically, the three courses were Dr. Richard Boland's courses, "Inquiry II: Inductive Ways of Knowing" and "Technology and Social System Design" and Dr. Bo Carlsson's course, "Business as a Dynamic System: The Evolution of Organizational Structure."

> **From a concept generation perspective, the lesson is to be patient. It is important to be patient and get the concept fully formed. It is also necessary to be patient in its adoption.**

Dr. Carlsson's course provided an insight into the framework of technological systems. The role of information was prominent in the growth of organizations (Chandler, 1990) and product innovation (Utterback, 1994). Of particular interest to me were the ideas of increasing economic returns due to the role of information (Arthur, 1990) and that the rise of technology was path dependent (David, 1992).

One of the objectives from the syllabus of Dr. Boland's course was to "re-theorize and recast a research question in alternative ways." For me, the course did just that. While wading through Giddens (1984) is not for the faint of heart, it gave me a great feel for large ideas. I "retheorized" his idea of substitution sets into the theory that information is a substitution for wasted physical resources. This theory underpins the concept of the Digital Twin.

From Kuhn (1996), I understood the importance (and difficulty) in paradigm shifts. This emphasized the importance of maturing the Digital Twin concept. Dr. Boland's other course introduced me to Simon

(1996), who understood the promise of modeling and simulation and led me to other giants in the information field.

My DM research was bifurcated from that point on. My primary goal was to finish the program by completing the required Advanced Research Project (ARP), so I selected a research question that I could conclude in the necessary time. I did not feel comfortable or confident that my information concepts were mature enough. My advisor, Dr. Boland, thought I should continue to pursue the ARP topic, but for me it was a means to an end.

At the same time, I was continuing my research into information. This led me to Turing (1950), Machlup (1983), Fauconnier (1994), Boulding (1966), and others. In particular, two books of collected essays (Lamberton 1996; Machlup & Mansfield 1983) were invaluable in helping me crystallize my ideas and concepts of the Digital Twin.

Summary and Conclusion

By the time I had graduated in 2000, I had concluded that information existed in its own right, separate and distinct from the physical objects it is embedded in. Information could be stripped from those physical objects and could be used in place of the requirement to physically possess those objects in order to interrogate its information. In fact, this information precedes the realization of a physical product. The ideal is that we want to create, test, manufacture, and support a product virtually. Only when we get it right do we physically make it. This is the Digital Twin concept.

From a concept generation perspective, the lesson is to be patient. It is important to be patient and get the concept fully formed. It is also necessary to be patient in its adoption. I remember Professor Boyatzis saying that good ideas can take a decade or more to develop and catch on. The Digital Twin is an example of that.

Keywords
Digital Twin, Physical Twin, Digital Twin Prototype, Digital Twin Instance, Digital Twin Aggregate

About the Author: Michael W. Grieves, DM

Dr. Grieves is an internationally renowned expert in Product Lifecycle Management (PLM) and originated the concept of the Digital Twin. He has consulted and/or done research at some of the top global organizations, including NASA, Boeing, and General Motors.

In addition to his academic credentials, Dr. Grieves has over four decades of extensive executive and deep technical experience in both global and entrepreneurial technology and manufacturing companies. He founded and took public a $100 million systems integration company and subsequently served as its audit and compensation committee chair. He is currently Chief Scientist of Advanced Manufacturing at Florida Tech.

Rachel Talton

In the nine years since I earned my DM degree, the personal transformation, expertise I have gained, and the DM degree itself have had significant impact on my practice.

The Currency of Trust: Elevating Engagement Through Integrity, Benevolence and Competence

My DM Journey

The first day I walked into the Doctor of Management office at Case Western Reserve University's Weatherhead School of Management, I was clear about what I wanted to accomplish. I was a moderately successful recovering executive banker who had lost my first husband Mark suddenly to a heart attack. Just finding my footing in the entrepreneurial space, I was involved with a wonderful new man in my life. My life was moving in the right direction; however, I had a provocative question that had bothered me since my early days as a business banker. During my time at the financial institution, I was extremely effective at attracting new business customers to the bank, but ultimately the customers would end up choosing another institution. They would come through the front door and leave out of the back door. Why was this happening and how could I work toward changing that?

I was positive about the possibilities of creating new knowledge. I was particularly interested in a topic that brought me joy and solved the problem of customer churn. Specifically, how can one create a beloved brand — a brand where consumer satisfaction and loyalty was aligned with institutional values? More importantly, a brand where each stakeholder's needs were being met, and the organization was able to grow in profitability *because they were meeting stakeholder needs.*

At the Weatherhead School, I had a wonderful discussion with Bo Carlsson, who was then the director of the Doctor of Management Program.

I told him about my desire to help companies create beloved brands that deliver customer value, employee satisfaction, and economic profitability. He nodded knowingly, likely thinking, *This young lady is certainly boiling the ocean, but she does have passion!*

After a year of study in the Doctor of Management (DM) Program, I understood that one cannot *create* love for a brand. Then I began to research triple bottom line, social corporate responsibility, psychological safety, diversity and inclusion and landed on research that explores how trust creates loyalty in brands and in leaders. The reason I landed on trust was twofold. First, I built a strong relationship with Dr. Jadgip Singh, a Fulbright Scholar in the area of trust, who happened to be our quantitative methods professor.

> **I was personally transformed by the very rigorous research, the relationships I built within our cohort, and the positive experience from the program.**

Secondly, after researching how emotional intelligence and integrity influences the bottom line in organizations, I found that although you cannot earn love, you could earn, nurture, and even repair trust.

Ultimately, I wrote my dissertation on the impact of trust and distrust on consumer value, satisfaction, and loyalty across three discrete industries: banking, hospitals, and retailers. The changing needs of consumers, a growing climate of distrust in the marketplace, and the proliferation of consumer access to information all presented the need for rigorous examination of strategic management practices. This research extended the relationship management literature and bridged the gap to institutional and functional theory literature; however, this work is only a beginning. In these tumultuous times, evidence shows that the industry environment has a significant impact on a firm's strategic ability to earn the loyalty of a key stakeholder group: its customer.

How Trust Transformed My Practice
In the nine years since I earned my DM degree, the personal transformation, expertise I have gained, and the DM degree itself have had significant impact on my practice. First, I would like to differentiate the knowledge and expertise from the degree. Weatherhead School of

Management is an excellent learning institution for the study of business management. I was able to expand my knowledge in the areas of trust and distrust and their impact on consumer loyalty. In addition, I was personally transformed by the very rigorous research, the relationships I built within our cohort, and the positive experience from the program.

Weatherhead is strong at transferring knowledge and it must continue to help define the market and the differences between a traditional PhD and a DM type of degree. Some helpful areas to think about in this differentiation include the following:

- The **DM practitioner-scholar** looks to make a contribution by applying or developing focal theory; the **traditional PhD scholar** seeks to make a contribution with generalized theory;
- The **DM practitioner-scholar** is a problem solver; the **traditional PhD scholar** is a theory developer;
- The **DM practitioner-scholar** asks how do I get over this hurdle? While the **traditional PhD scholar** asks, how do I understand and explain this hurdle better?
- The **DM practitioner-scholar** draws upon integrative education; the **traditional PhD scholar** draws upon highly specialized disciplinary education.

It is hoped that the DM alumni and the university will continue to partner to ensure that the corporate marketplace and academia understand the benefits of practitioner-scholarship. I know people continue to move these ideas forward and this is appreciated.

The knowledge I gained about trust (and distrust) and leadership has been used by my organization to transform the leaders and environments of many organizations, including Lbrands, Swagelok, AARP, PNC Bank, General Motors, Microsoft, Fisher Foods, and Unilever. Using our knowledge about trust, distrust, value creation, and loyalty, we help executives become transformational versus transactional and increase their ROI. Because much of our work involves marketing research, we can help organizations understand the value of creating trust in relationships and the quality of their products and services with their customers, their employees, their shareholders, and the marketplace overall.

One of the differentiators we used in my research is not only the development of trust, and the power of building trust in leadership, brand, product and services. It is also the *mitigation of distrust.* I found that managers across industry sectors attend to consumer distrust as they make strategic marketing and management decisions. If firms do not seek to both measure and alleviate distrust in addition to monitoring and building trust, the threat to their business may exceed any gains that establishing trust affords. In retail, managers would be well-served to consistently monitor the industry climate, as consumers are sensitive to fluctuations of trust and distrust at the industry-level, and reward or punish retailers based on their relationship management approach. In retail and hospitals, managers must be mindful that high industry distrust provides unique opportunities to drive loyalty in specific brands, while high industry trust should signal the requirement to immediately work to mitigate firm distrust. We find this to be true today, in fact, based on the 2019 Edelman Trust Survey, consumers ranked brand trust as one of the top factors they consider when making a purchase, with 81 percent of survey respondents saying that they "must be able to trust the brand to do what is right." In fact, according to the 2019 report, doing right by society can also boost sales. While 47 percent of consumers are able to trust a brand for its products alone, 55 percent report trusting a brand when it offers both a valuable product and treats its customers well. When positively impacting society is factored into the trust equation, the number of consumers inclined to side with a specific brand jumps to 68 percent. Interestingly, this is just as true today as it was 10 years ago when our research was first done. Perhaps more.

Here are some of the definitions I shared in my paper with Drs. Nick Berente and Jagdip Singh, *Winning Consumer Trust and Loyalty in Distrust Dominated Environments*, which are important as I translated them into practice to use currently with clients:

1. **Industry-level Trust** — observed or experienced skills, competencies, and characteristics that enable a party to have influence with some specific domain. Also, behaviors that reflect and underlying motivation place the consumer's interest ahead of self-interest (Sirdeshmukh, Singh, et. al., 2002). Finally, behaviors that reflect honesty, values, moral character and a set of ethical standards with which the trustee agrees (Grayson, Johnson & Chen, 2008). This is then repeated in our work as Firm-level Trust.

2. **Industry-level Distrust** — perceived skepticism that observed or experienced skills or competencies exist. Perceived doubt a high level of competence is exhibited in that industry. Additionally, behaviors that reflect the desire to put self-interest ahead of interest of consumers. Perceived doubt that benevolence toward the consumer exists (Sirdeshmukh, Singh, et. al., 2002). Finally, behaviors that reflect unethical behaviors, a lack of integrity and dishonestly (Grayson, Johnson & Chen, 2008). This is then repeated in our work as Firm-level Distrust.

3. **Firm-level Value** — the consumer's perception of the benefits minus the costs of maintaining an ongoing relationship with a service provider (Sirdeshmukh, Singh, et. al., 2002).

4. **Firm-level Satisfaction** — overall evaluation based on the total purchase and consumption experience with a good or service over time (Hallowell, 1996).

5. **Firm-level Loyalty** — percent of consumer purchases for a particular product or service that goes to a specific company or brand. Firms generally try to gain as much business as possible from each consumer (Zethamel, Berry & Parasuraman, 1990). Additionally, the consumer willingness to recommend a company, brand or product to family and friends (Reichheld, 2003). Finally, level of commitment to a company and an intention to purchase from that company (Harris & Goode, 2004).

These were main variables of interest in research that have now served me well as a consultant and maintaining my client base through empirically based ideas and definitions of the terminology helpful for gaining deeper insights into this space.

My practice operationalizes behaviors around trustworthiness, which has expanded our expertise in Diversity, Equity, and Inclusion. So often trust is broken, because of behaviors that violate the trust of women (with sexual harassment and worse), people of color (with racist and xenophobic behaviors and words), LGBTQ communities (with language and behaviors that are antithetical to honoring LGBTQ people), and that of many other marginalized groups. Our goal is to create authentic leaders, who understand diversity, equity, and inclusion. Then, we help them to create systems, which measure their success. Most importantly, we help companies design programs that tie diversity hires, the cultural climate, and inclusive leadership to executive and manager pay.

One of the ways we do this is to start executive coaching sessions, workshops, and training classes with a shared definition of trust and transformational leadership. We assess leadership style *and* the environment our participant's leadership style creates. We include rigorous work around implicit bias, modeling inclusive leadership, building authentic dialogue, shared vision and emotional intelligence, understanding privilege, ethical leadership, and using storytelling to create great leaders. We end exactly where we began — with trust and leadership — but with new behaviors, communication methods, measurements, and results available for these leaders to access.

Trust Forward, Always Forward

I mentioned three elements of the DM that had an impact on my life since graduating. The remaining two elements are the degree itself and my personal transformation. The degree itself has been important for me, but not overly significant, because I have not had an interest in academia as a profession. When I am asked about my research and where I earned my degree, people are interested in the area of trust, the process I took to gain my degree, and the university from which I earned it. When I decide to teach one day, the degree will take on another level of importance.

Finally, I have been personally transformed. This trust journey has been interesting and challenging, transformational, and tactical. First, I have been tactically transformed. In other words, I now know better how to communicate with people and how that communication may be heard and understood. I have a better insight into how to earn the trust of others, and how to teach them to earn trust. Much of this is just part of who you are, but knowing how others perceive these behaviors makes a difference in your ability be effective. There is a cost to distrust, and it is financial, social, cultural, and personal. If you learn to become trustworthy, and to trust others, the sustainable value your professional leadership and brand can attain is immeasurable.

Keywords
Trust, Leadership, Engagement, Inclusion, Marketing

About the Author: Rachel Talton, DM

Dr. Talton is CEO of Synergy, a brand strategy and marketing research consultancy. Synergy's proprietary process aligns the Six Dimensions of Brand Experience (BloomPrint™) using rigorous research, and resulting in dramatically improved long-term corporate profitability — and customer passion. In addition to Dr. Talton's success as an entrepreneur, she is a sought-after keynote speaker, executive coach, author and scholar. She also serves on the Board of Directors of Destination Cleveland, Cuyahoga Community College Foundation, the Akron Community Foundation and the JumpStart, Inc. Inclusion Committee. She is a member of the Cleveland Bridge Builders Class of 2002, as well as the Leadership Cleveland Class of 2005. Dr. Talton is also CTO (Chief Transformation Officer) of Flourish Leadership, LLC and the Flourish Conference for Women in Leadership

Dr. Talton earned her Doctorate in Management from Case Western Reserve University's Weatherhead School of Management, where she also served as Adjunct Professor of Marketing. Her research is focused on the impact of perceptions of trust, satisfaction, and value on consumer loyalty in dynamic-industry environments. She holds an MBA with a concentration in Finance from Cleveland State University, as well as a BA in Psychology. She is a lifetime member of the Beta Gamma Sigma International Business Honor Society. Rachel's personal passions include international travel, community service and public speaking.

Michael Fisher

Seeking to understand the drivers of viral growth, as part of my doctoral research in the Doctor of Management (DM) program at Case Western Reserve University (CWRU), I undertook the study of different social media networks.

The Power of
Consumer Misbehavior

Computer scientist Tom Kilburn is responsible for writing the world's very first piece of software, which was run at 11:00 AM on June 21st, 1948, at the University of Manchester in England (Copeland, 2000). Kilburn and his colleague Freddie Williams had built one of the earliest computers, the Manchester Small-Scale Experimental Machine (SSEM) and programmed it to perform mathematical calculations (Copeland, 2011). For decades after this groundbreaking event, computers were programmed with punch cards in which holes denoted specific machine code instructions. Many early programming languages, including Fortran, Cobol, and the various IBM assembler languages were programmed in this manner. Eventually this gave way to other interfaces for developing computer programs including the terminal and keyboard.

A decade after the first program, John Tukey coined the word "software" in a 1958 article about computer programming (Shapiro, 2000). While the origin of the term "software engineer" is not clear, many articles claim that the term was coined in the Fall of 1968 at the Garmisch-Partenkirchen conference (Andelfinger, 2002). The term, it is said, was a challenge to the software community to get its act together and start rationalizing the software production process. The need for this spurn was what later became known as the "software crisis."

The early days of computer programming were noted for the difficulty of writing useful and efficient computer programs in the required time. The software crisis was originally defined in terms of productivity, but it evolved to emphasize quality as well, since bad software was responsible for everything from property damage to even the loss of life (Levenson, 1995). With the increase in the complexity of the software, many problems arose because existing development methods were insufficient.

Practitioners and scholars from the 1970s through the 1990s trumpeted various tools, formal methods, and processes as silver bullets. Tools included structured programming languages such as Ada and object-oriented programming languages such as C++. Formal methods included the Capability Maturity Model (CMM) and Information Technology Infrastructure Library (ITIL). Introduced processes included the waterfall software development methodology and the Unified Process based on Unified Modeling Language (UML). The waterfall methodology allowed for a sequential design approach for software engineering. In 1985, the United States Department of Defense captured this approach in DOD-STD-2167A, defining standards for working with software development contractors, which stated that "the contractor shall implement a software development cycle that includes the following six phases: Preliminary Design, Detailed Design, Coding and Unit Testing, Integration, and Testing". Brooks (1986) argued that no individual tool, method, or process would ever make a 10-fold improvement in productivity within 10 years.

The rise of the Internet led to very rapid growth in demand for software in many smaller organizations, which highlighted the need for simpler, faster methodologies for getting from requirements to deployment, quicker, and easier. This era introduced agile software development methodologies such as scrum and kanban. The term agile was popularized by the Manifesto for Agile Software Development, which espoused 12 principles for software development such as, "Our highest priority is to satisfy the customer through early and continuous delivery of valuable software." While agile has been hailed as a much better methodology for modern software development, it too has failed to meet the mark as a silver bullet.

The Internet also introduced the ability for consumer-based companies to achieve the holy-grail of marketing, viral growth. Essentially, viral marketing is a variant of word of mouth marketing, in which consumers disseminate commercial messages on behalf of the company (Salminen

& Hytönen, 2012). Seeking to understand the drivers of viral growth, as part of my doctoral research in the Doctor of Management (DM) program at Case Western Reserve University (CWRU), I undertook the study of different social media networks. Some of these included the failed Friendster that was only able to amass eight million users, as well as the still very successful Facebook, with over two billion users.

Our research on viral growth determined that the social networks that allowed customers to best reflect their self-identity were the winners. Often this required the social networking companies to allow users to misbehave with their products or use the product in a manner that it was not intended in order for the user to best display their self-identity. An example of two antithetical responses to users misbehaving in order to more fully display their self-identities is how Friendster and Facebook responded when customers began creating accounts for their pets. Friendster management acted to swiftly shut down the accounts while Facebook managers enthusiastically supported the development of dogbook and catbook applications, resulting in over one million pet users by 2010 (Fisher, 2013). Based on our research, we published a book, *The Power of Customer Misbehavior: Drive Growth and Innovation by Learning from Your Customers* (Fisher, Abbott, & Lyytinen, 2013), which encouraged consumer-based companies to co-create with their customers by watching how they really use the product and not assume they do so how it was intended.

This concept of developing a culture within a software engineering organization that allows or even encourages customers to use products to solve problems other than what they were originally planned for has been adopted as the newest iteration of software development methodology, beyond agile. The concept of encouraging customer misbehavior based on our research has been implemented as part of a newly defined discovery process for software engineering.

Etsy, like dozens of other tech companies, has implemented a Product Development Culture program based in part on Marty Cagan's methodology for product development outlined in his book, *INSPIRED: How to Create Tech Products Customers Love.* As Cagan (2017) states in the introduction,

"...there are many people looking for a recipe for product success — a prescriptive guide or framework to how to create products customers love...the unfortunate truth is that's just not how great products are created. It is much more important to create the right product culture for success, and understand the array of product discovery and delivery techniques..." (p. xviii).

Marty has dedicated a full chapter to the Power of Customer Misbehavior as a methodology to identifying customer needs. Cagan (2007) states,

"Historically, there are two main approaches used by good teams to come up with product opportunities...try to assess market opportunities...or look at what technology or data enable...However, some of the most successful companies today have taken a third approach...allow, and even encourage, our customers to use our products, to solve problems other than what we planned for and officially support" (p. 217–218).

Our research team is incredibly proud that our insights have helped in a small part to usher in a new era of software engineering that is focused on introducing cultural changes that are critical to building great consumer based products and not focused on the methodological steps and ceremonies that are central to agile software development processes. While this new approach is also not necessarily a silver bullet to the software crisis that has existed now for nearly half a century, it does provide a marked improvement for software engineering.

Keywords
Consumer Misbehavior, Computer Programming, Culture,
Consumer-Based Products

About the Author: Michael Fisher, PhD

Dr. Fisher is currently Etsy's Chief Technology Officer. Prior to joining Etsy, he was co-founder of the consulting firm AKF Partners. He has held a variety of technology leadership roles including CTO of Quigo (acquired by AOL) and VP, Engineering & Architecture for PayPal. He served as an officer and pilot in the US Army.

Dr. Fisher received a PhD and an MBA from Case Western Reserve University's Weatherhead School of Management and served as an Adjunct Professor in the Design & Innovation department. He co-authored two books on technology scalability that have been translated into five languages both with second editions, and a third book based on his research of customer growth.

Solange Charas

The rigor of the program developed new competencies so that I was able to research and learn different theories and apply them successfully in these collaborations. This is critical as it is what now differentiates my approach and deliverables from other practitioners.

Why the DM Program Made a Difference

Every successful professional with many years of practitioner and senior management experience has a different reason for undertaking the commitment to go back to school — that was certainly clear in my cohort. Some went back to school to pivot their careers, some to deepen their competencies to advance in their careers, and some to explore a specific question. My reasons were three-fold: to satisfy my passion of learning, to fulfill a goal of obtaining a terminal degree, and to gain the competencies to amplify my impact on the business community. In evaluating different programs, I deliberately chose a "brick-and-mortar" program because I wanted the benefit of interacting with members of a cohort — to be able to appreciate their reasons for returning to school and learn from their past experience, perspectives, and research process, both in the classroom, and more importantly, in those informal and memorable moments outside of class.

It would be easy to say that the Doctor of Management (DM) Program exposed me to academic resources (e.g., professors, colleagues) and a research discipline (understanding academic articles, designing and conducting qualitative and quantitative research) embedded in the actual "study" of topics in the curriculum and end it there, as that is the promise of the program. However, the experience has had a more profound impact — it transformed the way I think and approach problems. For example, in the years since defending my thesis, I have participated in several research collaborations — most of which have been in an area outside of my focus. The rigor of the program allowed me to develop new competencies so that I was able to research and learn different theories and apply them successfully in these collaborations. This is critical as it is what now differentiates my approach and deliverables from other practitioners.

In sum, the program has given me the confidence to be bold about combining theory and practice and seeing business problems from an original and unique perspective — with the goal of promoting business sustainability.

My Journey

I was successful in accomplishing all of my objectives for returning to school — what was unexpected was how my experience in the program manifested in my post-program future. After graduating, my plans had been to go back into consulting as a "solopreneur," or to join an organization in an HR role with one more credential and "tools" to be effective and efficient — to elevate my contribution to business success by bringing into the practitioners' world the discipline and rigor of the academic world.

What actually happened was quite unexpected:

1. **I became an educator at NYU, USC, and Columbia in their respective Master's Programs.** This has brought me a new kind of personal and professional satisfaction that I had not experienced before, nor ever imagined I would. I have contributed to not only these institutions (e.g., designing curricula) but to the hundreds of students I have touched. What is unexpected is what I am teaching and to whom: Quantitative Methods and Models and Finance to HR students. Traditionally viewed as a "soft-side" profession, I am helping to transform this "subjective" decision-driven function to an "objective"/ quantitative decision-driven function by exposing current and future HR professionals to a new way of thinking about their role and their function — expanding the understanding of impact on the business through incorporating financial and quantitative skills in managing the people side of the business.

2. **I became a thought leader/influencer:**
    a. I have been published/cited in more than 150 articles in practitioner publications and cited in 25 academic works. The subject matter of much I have written has been primarily focused on sustain-

able management systems — and in bridging what academics research and how practitioners apply this research. For example, my research focused on board room dynamics as a driver of economic value creation. I believe my research was the first of its kind to gather primary data on the director's experience of "team." Today, this concept of teamwork and boardroom dynamics is gaining prominence in the practitioner's approach to building effective boards (e.g., screening and selection, governance quality).

b. I have collaborated with other academics to further the impact of the scholarly-practitioner mindset, including those at University of Georgia and Morehouse College and our papers were presented at academic conferences. A future collaboration with Dr. Adrian Wolfberg is being planned that will combine Adrian's insight into the decision-making process of military generals with my insight in how decisions are made in the boardroom (Wolfberg, 2017).

c. In addition, I am a champion of including women in the boardroom and in C-suite management (serving on the Board of The Thirty Percent Coalition). In the last several years, we have influenced more than 180 public companies to add a woman to their board (30% Coalition, 2019), and we have seen California (Senate Bill 826) and Illinois (House Bill 3394) pass laws enacting board diversity.

d. In January 2019, I joined The Conference Board as one of eight Distinguished Principal Research Fellows — an opportunity that would not have been possible without my PhD and an opportunity to have an impact on thought leadership in the business community.

I started a business that employs people: Perhaps the most exciting and unexpected event resulting from my Case degree is that I have started a new business — specifically to bring a more quantitative and evidence-based approach to human capital decision-making. This is a direct result of my academic experience. In the past five years, there has been a groundswell of interest in the intersection between data analytics and human resources — surprising since this discipline has traditionally shunned "numbers." This acknowledgment that human capital is a significant driver of firm performance culminated in March 2019 with the SEC's pronouncement that they will be viewing human resources as an intangible asset (versus a cost) and will soon be issuing guidelines on human capital disclosure. In the academic community, this is not a new concept (Adelowotan & Olaoluniyi, 2015; Becker & Huselid, 2006; Hajrullina & Romadanova, 2014). But that it is now being adopted in the practitioners' world is a testament to the "scholarly practitioner" perspective acceptance. The person who presented to the SEC was a scholarly practitioner (Coates, 2019). This view that human capital is an intangible asset will have far-reaching ramifications not just for public companies, but also for all organizations, and, most importantly, in realigning how human capital is realized for accounting and tax purposes. I intend to be at the forefront of this movement — something prior to the PhD, I would not have had the knowledge base nor the confidence to do.

Keywords
Human Capital, Decision Making, Business Sustainability, Education

About The Author: Solange Charas, PhD
Dr. Charas is the Founder and CEO of HCMoneyball — an analytics SaaS solution to enhance decision-making around investments in human capital programs. She consults to corporations, boards of directors and investors. She has been Chief HR Officer for three public companies and served as a Board Director for two (Chairperson of the Audit and Remuneration Committees). Dr. Charas is an adjunct Professor at Columbia, USC, and NYU.

Daniel Cohen

Entering CWRU's DM program turned out to be a great experience and, as this story unfolds, what resulted will have a significant impact on theory and practice on a global level. Had I not gone to CWRU, my method would have been confined to the borders of my classroom and lab at Cornell and would have had a limited impact on the field of entrepreneurship.

How Learning in a Unique Doctoral Program Transformed a Classroom Approach into an Empirically Proven Method for Developing Innovative Opportunities

Twelve years ago, I founded eLab, Cornell University's startup accelerator program, and taught entrepreneurship courses at the undergraduate and MBA level. I had recently transitioned to academia after a successful run as an entrepreneur that included co-founding, scaling, and effectively exiting after 15 years. My academic title was Senior Lecturer, and my focus was teaching and program building. Since the mission of the accelerator program was to launch startups, helping students spot, evaluate, and select high potential entrepreneurial opportunities became strategically important to me. In addition, teaching entrepreneurial courses often includes instructing students about opportunity identification. Being an entrepreneur by background, spotting valuable opportunities came naturally to me. I was somewhat dismayed by the fact that when I asked students to find valuable ideas, they came back with ideas that were, frankly, not so valuable.

I began to ponder why opportunity identification came more easily to seasoned entrepreneurs and why this task was such a struggle for nascent entrepreneurs. I reasoned that this was a problem worth solving since most nascent entrepreneurs do not end up becoming entrepreneurs in practice (Farmer et al., 2011). Markets can be cold. If you bring something to the world that is not valuable or does not solve a problem for customers, markets will quickly let an entrepreneur know they are off track. Armed with poor quality opportunities that do not receive market validation, nascent entrepreneurs may wrongly conclude that they do not have what it takes to succeed as an entrepreneur and may choose to pursue another career (Markowska et al., 2015). Further, the United States (US) is seeing a reduction in entrepreneurial activity amongst people under the age of 40 (Simon & Barr, 2015). Given that entrepreneurial activity has a significant impact on job creation, economic growth, and GDP, this problem was one that needed to be addressed.

I began to solve this problem qualitatively by talking to my students and asking them about their approach to spotting, evaluating, and selecting high potential opportunities. I sensed that, due to a lack of work experience and domain expertise, they were solving their own organic problems. The general approach to teaching ideation was to ask students to keep an active log where they could record problems they noted and later brainstorm potential solutions as a group assignment in class (Detienne & Chandler, 2004). The problems they encountered were often narrow-minded and tethered to their campus life experience, limiting applicability and potential to scale to other markets. I also talked to professors who taught entrepreneurship and asked them their opinions about the ability of students to generate valuable entrepreneurial opportunities. These professors generally concluded that most students were not able to spot valuable opportunities or to execute on the idea and build successful companies. However, universities, perhaps motivated to help uncover the next Facebook or Google on campus, were investing heavily in entrepreneurship education causing entrepreneurship education to grow at an enormous pace over the past 20 years (Neck, 2016). I had uncovered a significant problem of practice: universities had invested significantly in entrepreneurship programs, centers, curriculum, faculty hiring, and accelerator or incubator programs while student entrepreneurs were struggling to spot, evaluate, and select high potential entrepreneurial opportunities. At the same time, professors seemed to agree that students lacked experience and did not have enough domain expertise to generate high potential opportunities. However, some significant successes, such as Facebook and Google, along with enough other successful dorm room startups gave me pause. What if the students are capable but are simply lacking an effective method or a new approach?

I embarked on this problem of practice the way any conscientious teacher would — by standing on the shoulders of scholars and practitioners who had preceded me. I read Scott Shane's excellent book *Find-*

ing Fertile Ground (Shane, 2004), where I learned that change is a key driver of entrepreneurial opportunities. Shane (2004) mentions four critical areas of change that he deems fertile ground for finding entrepreneurial opportunities: social and demographic changes, technological change, legal and regulatory change, and changes in industry structure. Shane (2004) reasoned that established companies win most of the time because they have negotiated a learning curve by working consistently in an industry over time and having to meet customer needs continuously. All of their investments are in the current operation, approach, technology, training of employees, etc. When things change, no one has gone through the learning curve and new opportunities start to favor nimble startups that can take advantage of opportunities that emerged due to the change. I began to assign Shane's (2004) book in my classes, but my students, while appreciating the central premise of the book, had difficulty connecting with the ideas they were creating. While they could see that change leads to opportunity for those who anticipate their arrival, they still thought of those ideas as suited for others — particularly others with more experience. The McMullen and Shepherd (2006)

> **When I began the CWRU program, I learned to think critically. The first step, as I quickly learned, involved learning how to do a thorough, high-quality literature review.**

article explains this phenomenon as the difference between a third-person opportunity (an opportunity for someone else) and a first-person opportunity (an opportunity for me). This approach generated many third-person ideas — good quality ideas — and yet the students often could not conceptualize pursuing these ideas. Further, while they appreciated Shane's (2004) book, they often struggled to see opportunities that could result from changes beyond the examples laid out in the book. I started to search for real-life examples of the changes that Shane (2004) referenced and began to create exercises and examples designed to help students search for opportunities in these four areas of change.

I read Detienne and Chandler's (2004) article on a new method of teaching opportunity identification known as the SEEC method. I was impressed that they had invented their own technique of teaching opportunity identification and had rigorously tested it empirically.

Using this method, they found significant results indicating increased quantity of opportunities spotted and innovativeness of the ideas. I adopted some parts of the SEEC method into my teaching approach. This method asked students to keep a problem log and to record problems they had encountered in daily activities. Students would then brainstorm solutions to these problems during class activities. While I was impressed with the number of ideas generated using this method, I found that most of the problems identified were campus-oriented such as issues with campus parking, creating an app to find a seat in the library, campus food quality, or a myriad of other problems. This method yielded an opposite outcome of Shane's approach — too many first-person opportunities that were narrow-minded and not so valuable.

I read James Fiet's (2002) book on using a systematic search to uncover entrepreneurial opportunity. Fiet (2002) reasoned that passive search (the notion that ideas are out there just waiting to be found) might not work so well for nascent entrepreneurs as it does for more seasoned entrepreneurs. Instead, a more active search approach would perhaps be more suited to nascent entrepreneurs who lack work experience and domain expertise. According to Baron (2006), experienced entrepreneurs think differently than inexperienced entrepreneurs and use pattern recognition to connect the dots between their previous work experience, domain expertise, previous entrepreneurial experience, and their professional network. Baron and Ensley (2006) found that experienced entrepreneurs assess opportunities almost immediately by estimating potential profits or profit margins, while nascent entrepreneurs focus more on novelty and are not as concerned with profits or margins.

Starting with my expertise and cobbling together bits and pieces I had learned from scholars in the field as well as other practicing entrepreneurs, I created a method of teaching nascent entrepreneurs how to spot valuable opportunities. It was a trial and error approach, and it took time, reflection, failure, more trial, and learning, but eventually this method began to bear fruit and valuable opportunities began to hatch with ever growing and consistent frequency. More and more valuable ideas came out of my classes, and the eLab Accelerator program spawned many successful startups that raised $150M in venture capital. Anecdotally, the method was sound, and I had refined it into a successful approach in the classroom and the lab. At this point in my career, I decided to earn a PhD. I found that the Doctor of Management (DM) program at Case Western Reserve University (CWRU) had a flexible format designed to fit in with a full-time career. I was enjoying my teaching and directing eLab and wanted to continue those activities instead of pursuing a PhD. exclusively. Entering CWRU's DM program turned out to be a great experience and, as this story unfolds, what resulted will have a significant impact on theory and practice on a global level. Had I not gone to CWRU, my method would have been confined to the borders of my classroom and lab at Cornell and would have had a limited impact on the field of entrepreneurship. Before the program, I did not have the knowledge or skill set to turn this into a scalable method capable of replication nor did I know how to rigorously test this method in order to identify its effects beyond anecdote.

The CWRU DM Program Effect
When I began the CWRU program, I learned to think critically. The first step, as I quickly learned, involved learning how to do a thorough, high-quality literature review. While my dissertation was on a different topic, I took my literature review skills and read deeply on opportunity identification. I read all of the articles in quality journals, and I began to assemble a method that could be replicated and taught by other professors. The next key learning involved developing skills, both qualitatively and quantitatively, to rigorously test hypotheses or make credible propositions. For my dissertation, I learned how to do time series analysis and growth modeling, which helped me to understand longitudinal research designs and how to measure change over time. This fundamental knowledge gave me the foundation necessary to learn how to conduct an experiment after I concluded the program at CWRU. In short, after completing the program at CWRU, I knew how to construct this into a replicable method that could be empirically tested to determine whether its effect could span beyond anecdote or the confines of my classroom and lab.

IDEATE Method in Action
The six distinct steps of the IDEATE framework are discussed here and illustrated in Appendix A.

The first step is 'Identify.' In this step, learners are taught how to identify a problem worth solving — to solve a pain point, a 'migraine headache' problem, rather than a matter of inconvenience or a 'nice to have' item (e.g., rather sell aspirin than vitamins). This step is accomplished by coaching learners to distinguish between exemplars, both valuable, high-quality opportunities and poor-quality opportunities so they can begin to develop proficiency in distinguishing between the two. Challenges to generating valuable or innovative opportunities, such as identifying problems for very small markets or problems that are simply feature enhancements to existing products, are discussed. Instructors list several of these exemplars (e.g., an App that alerts students when the gym is less crowded or the virtual student ID card that replaces the frequently misplaced physical card) and stress why the problem is not valuable or innovative.

The second step, labeled 'Discover,' focuses on where and how to actively search for opportunities in fertile areas or problem-rich environments. Classroom exercises encourage learners to explore activities about which they are passionate. When they are avidly involved in activities, it is natural to notice 'migraine headache' problems or unmet needs. Students are also encouraged to probe their life experiences, such as studying abroad, in order to help them uncover opportunities, which they have been exposed to in other environments that might have appeal in other markets. While this step can be similar to the process of passive search, IDEATE learners are challenged to come up with a second set of 10 opportunities to address 'migraine headache' type problems.

In the third step, learners are taught ways to 'Enhance' opportunities (e.g., adding an innovative twist) to create a more valuable solution for potential customers. The key to this section is to teach learners how to improve the quality of opportunities to make them more valuable. Instructors propose a real scenario that explains an existing product or service that students are not familiar with and ask learners to increase the value proposition of the product or service. After task completion, learners are informed about how the entrepreneur actually improved the product. Once several examples of ways to improve opportunities generated by others are discussed, learners are asked to enhance opportunities they have searched for and create an additional cluster of 10 opportunities.

In the fourth step, labeled 'Anticipate,' specific types of change likely to yield future entrepreneurial opportunities are discussed. There are four types of change known to be fertile ground for entrepreneurial opportunity (Shane, 2004): social and demographic change, technological change, political and regulatory change, and changes in industry structure. For each type of change, students are prompted with specific examples and then have to anticipate customer needs that will result from these changes. For instance, one prompt for social and demographic change is the aging society in the United States. Students are asked to generate opportunities emerging as a result of this specific change. Subsequently, students are asked to research each of these areas of change and anticipate what opportunities will likely emerge that are worth pursuing. While students have remarked that this section alone can account for one hundred or more valuable opportunities, they must only generate a fourth set of ten new opportunities at this point.

The fifth step focuses on the way to 'Target,' by exploring the customer base most likely to want to purchase and support a new opportunity. This step helps to develop clarity as to who the customer is and why he/she might buy the proposed product or service. The exercises in this section begin by asking learners to describe, in detail, the target market customer for various products. Then, after sharpening their focus, learners turn their attention back to their own opportunities and describe the target market customers. Having just completed the 'Enhance' and 'Anticipate' sections, students are prompted to consider other needs these target market customers may have as an additional source of ten new opportunities. After the fifth step, students should have a list of 50 opportunities. Students conduct evaluations (in step six below) on the first 50 opportunities identified (10 ideas for each of the preceding five sections) and then, after being fully immersed in the IDEATE method, are tasked with generating 50 more opportunities to reach the 100 opportunities identified.

The sixth and final step is 'Evaluate,' in which learners complete a rubric to score, select, and defend identified opportunities. The evaluation rubric has two parts. Part one is a quick evaluation tool that asks students, on a scale from 1 to 5, to estimate the degree to which the problem they are solving is a 'migraine headache' problem rather than a simple matter of inconvenience. This score is then multiplied by a rating of 1 to 5, indicating their passion for each opportunity. This evaluation rubric includes criteria used by venture capitalists that have been empirically proven to increase the selection of valuable ideas. The top 10 opportunities identified through the 'multiplication exercise' above are then more deeply evaluated by conducting an internet search (e.g., Google search) to explore whether others are occupying this same competitive space. If the online search yields competition (a common occurrence), the learner needs to show meaningful differentiation in their product or service offering relative to this competition. The evaluation process also examines important issues such as profit potential, size of the target market, and the ability to protect the opportunity from competitors via barriers to entry. A final step in the evaluation phase (after the 100 ideas are culled to the ten most valuable ones), calls for students to engage in customer discovery where students interview selected target market customers to gain deeper insights into the nature of their problem and their interest in solving it. The feedback obtained through the 'customer discovery' process, serves to pare down the top ten ideas to the final three opportunities. Students are required to submit a description of these three opportunities (ranked from first to third) as a graded assignment.

Condensed Methodology

I created a natural experiment where the IDEATE method was taught in three courses, and the previous gold standard for teaching opportunity identification was taught in three other classes. The first module of the course pertained to opportunity identification, which was based on the previous gold standard, and took about five weeks, all of which were dedicated to opportunity identification. In the treatment group, the instructors were asked to teach opportunity identification using the IDEATE method for the same amount of time — the first five weeks in the semester. The course was the same with the same instructors and the same teaching material in the first five weeks for the two semesters. The major difference is the teaching method of opportunity identification.

In both semesters, students were surveyed at the beginning of the course (T1) and at the end of the opportunity identification module (T2). A total of 192 students participated in the study at T1 and 187 students participated at T2. Student responses at T1 and T2 were matched for the final analysis. After attrition and removing missing values, the final sample contained 149 respondents, of which 82 (55%) were female and 60 (40.3%) had an entrepreneur in their immediate family. The average age was 20.4, ranging from 19 to 24.

Main Hypothesis and Condensed Results

Hypothesis 1 (H1): Compared to the individuals trained in the passive search approach, those trained in the IDEATE method will generate more innovative opportunities.

While the level of innovativeness should range from 1 to 6 (the endpoints of the Likert scale), the maximum value in the data was only 3.67. This was because students selected and submitted three opportunities, and very few students had excellent quality (i.e., innovativeness) on all three opportunities identified. The correlation between the IDEATE measure and degree of innovativeness of opportunities was strong (ρ = .306; p < .01), and indicated that, when nothing was controlled for, there was a positive relationship between the two variables, providing preliminary support for H1.

To further test H1, Ordinary Least Square (OLS) was utilized. Model 1 contained the two control variables. Model 2 added the independent variable and the IDEATE training vs. the passive search training. The IDEATE treatment strongly and positively predicted innovativeness of opportunities (β = .309, p < .01). Additionally, IDEATE uniquely explained 10% of the variance ($\Delta R2$ = .10) in innovativeness of opportunities, thus fully supporting H1.

Conclusion: Impact of IDEATE

With strong empirical support in hand, the IDEATE method experiment paper is under second round review at a top tier academic journal. Further, the IDEATE method is being written as a field book and will be published internationally by Sage in January 2020.

Keywords

Experiment, Opportunity Identification, Teaching Method, Empirical Evidence

About the Author: Daniel Cohen, PhD

After a successful 15-year career as an entrepreneur that included founding, growing, and ultimately selling his startup, Dr. Cohen transitioned to academia full time in 2005 when he accepted a faculty appointment at The University of Iowa's Tippie College of Business from 2005–2007. While at the University of Iowa, Dr. Cohen earned accolades for teaching, advising and mentoring excellence before moving on to Cornell University from 2007 to 2015. While at Cornell, he taught courses on entrepreneurship and business at the undergraduate, graduate, and executive levels and founded and directed eLab — Cornell's entrepreneurship accelerator program hailed by Forbes Magazine as a major driver of Cornell's ascent to a #4 national ranking in entrepreneurship. Professor Cohen was also awarded Cornell's Robert N. Stern Memorial Award for Mentoring Excellence in 2012.

In 2015, Dr. Cohen moved on to Wake Forest University as a Full Professor of Practice in business and entrepreneurship. In 2016, Cohen co-founded Startup Lab and became more integrally involved in the Center for Innovation, Creativity and Entrepreneurship. In the summer of 2017, he was named the John C. Whitaker, Jr. Executive Director of the newly minted Center for Entrepreneurship while remaining a full Professor of Practice in Entrepreneurship. In terms of research, Dr. Cohen studies how nascent entrepreneurs develop passion for entrepreneurship and how, and under what conditions, they form an entrepreneurial identity. Dr. Cohen also researches how entrepreneurs develop key capabilities such as how to spot and develop valuable opportunities.

Appendix A

IDENTIFY

Teach students to differentiate between 'headache' problems with a clear value proposition that customers will pay to solve versus more myopic problems with ambiguous value propositions. Using a series of exercises, students learn what makes an opportunity valuable and worth pursuing.

DEMYSTIFY

We demystify entrepreneurship by engaging students in exercises that highlight less famous (but valuable) startups that spotted and solved headache problems for customers.

ENHANCE

Entrepreneurs begin to actively search for valuable ideas by focusing on enhancing existing ones.

ANTICIPATE

Successful entrepreneurs seem to understand the future better than most. If change leads to entrepreneurial opportunity, then entrepreneurs can study changes and anticipate what they will yield in terms of valuable ideas.

TARGETING THE MOST ZEALOUS CUSTOMERS

Ideas need validation from paying customers in order to be sustainable. With the IDEATE method, validation comes from early adopters most likely to resonate with the ideas.

EVALUATE

Evaluate and select the best idea. The evaluation component of the IDEATE method provides a rubric for student entrepreneurs to evaluate ideas in terms of the extent to which an idea solves a 'headache' problem, the size of the target market, the interest of the target market, the degree of personal interest in the idea, and the skills and abilities of the entrepreneur.

"You may say that I'm a dreamer, but I'm not the only one, I hope someday you'll join us and the world will be as one."

John Lennon

Dreamer

Having the desire to
improve the world with
a strong moral compass

R. Robertson Hilton

*I discovered that I was woefully unqualified
for the responsibilities and aspirations that
I had taken on. A careful search for an
educational program that could help me
climb the learning curve in a structured
manner led me to Weatherhead. To this day,
I consider myself extremely fortunate.*

Perfect Timing for a
New Model of Care

The Doctor of Management (DM) degree positioned me to contribute substantively to the field of aging at a critical time in two notable ways. First, as a direct result of my third year research paper, I engaged researchers and practitioners in defining a new model of caring for low-income seniors: affordable senior housing with services. Second, I launched the biennial Global Aging Network Applied Research Forums to expose practitioners from all over the world to research in aging outside of their countries.

Background

I entered the Program in the fall of 2002 to jump-start a second career in aging with the McGregor Foundation after working in banking and corporate finance for 27 years. Tracing our history back to 1877 and based in East Cleveland — Ohio's "worst" inner city urban area — McGregor stands among Cleveland's most venerable not-for-profits. When I joined the Board in the mid 90's, we cared for around 100 seniors in two buildings with an endowment exceeding $100 million — clearly a gross underutilization of our financial resources. As Board Chair in 1999, I engaged consultants to help us determine how to optimize the use of our endowment. The consultants recommended a bold strategy that included aggressive expansion and diversification of our services and facilities, establishing a grant-making foundation, and hiring a CEO with a business background. After conducting an unsuccessful nationwide search for the CEO, I decided to take the job myself in May 2001.

We adopted the mission of "supporting seniors in need and those who serve them." However, despite my Chicago MBA, career in finance, and having served for nearly 10 years on McGregor's board, I discovered that I was woefully unqualified for the responsibilities and aspirations that I had taken on. A careful search for an educational program that could help me climb the learning curve in a structured manner led me to Weatherhead. To this day, I consider myself extremely fortunate.

The launch of my new career and enrollment in the DM Program also came at a critical, if not alarming, time in the field of aging. The frantic realization that we as a nation were completely unprepared for the aging of the largest population bulge in our history, the "boomers," entered public policy for the first time. In Ohio, we fretted that expenditures on Medicaid might surpass the State's education budget. Today, it has. In Cleveland, we worried that residents aged 65 and over might someday exceed those aged 21 and under. They have. In addition, a survey commissioned by McGregor determined that the shortfall in "acceptable" housing for low-income seniors in Cuyahoga County exceeded 30,000 units.

Just as important, however, we realized that we really did not know how to care for vulnerable seniors so that they could enjoy the experience of aging, a period that for some claimed nearly 30% of their total lifespan. Few research studies actually engaged seniors as opposed to simply observing them. We did not know how seniors themselves defined "successful aging." Low-income seniors who could no longer live alone lived either in nursing homes, where they did not want to be, or under the care of a (usually female) family member. They had no other options. However, how could we devise solutions for the critical challenge of serving especially low-income seniors without their participation? A research question emerged as follows, what are the factors of successful aging from the viewpoint of seniors themselves? How do low-income seniors describe the "lived experience" of aging successfully?

Affordable Senior Housing with Services

As a result of my qualitative research, completed in the fall of 2003, I was surprised that the phenomenon that emerged over all others in the lives of the seniors I interviewed was "fear." I encountered fear of isolation, cognitive loss, financial ruin, declining health, loss of lifestyle preferences, and purpose. Nevertheless, if I was to design a new model of care to hopefully replace nursing homes and abusive home care, I needed to understand which of those "fears" were most critical to address, especially for low-income seniors.

For my quantitative study, I flipped the phenomenon of "fear" into the more positive construct of "wellness." I felt that seniors would be more responsive when surveyed about "wellness" than asking them about their "fears." Promoting wellness in transforming caregiving would certainly inspire more innovative solutions than a focus on dispelling fear.

I was fortunate to have developed business relationships with owner/ operators of affordable independent senior housing facilities across the country. With their assistance, I distributed more than 1,300 questionnaires to the residents of a random selection of my associates' properties. At each building, I offered a drawing for a $25 Walmart gift certificate to those residents who completed questionnaires. As a result, I enjoyed an extraordinary response rate.

The response to my survey identified three types of "wellness" as most important: social, cognitive, and lifestyle preferences. I was surprised that health and financial wellness did not score more highly. It appeared that residents of low-income senior housing have all of their financial needs met through government subsidized food and housing security programs. In addition, respondents seemed to differentiate between conventional good health and lifestyle preferences; that is, certain lifestyle preferences such as drinking and smoking are decidedly unhealthy but greatly valued by some seniors never the less. The underlying message in all of these discoveries was that seniors have their own ideas about "successful aging" that were not necessarily consistent with conventional research at the time.

An additional discovery was that facilities that are most responsive to the needs and preferences of their senior residents prove most successful in enabling residents to "age in place" rather than transferring to institutional care. Facilities achieve this by connecting each resident to the community resources they require to age successfully. Many employ "resident service coordinators" to facilitate these connections. This model, where services are brought to seniors to enable them to age in place, is the opposite of the nursing home model where seniors are brought to services. An additional advantage of this model is that it is less expensive to access services only as a resident needs them when the resident needs them. A nursing home, on the other hand, must incur the expense of permanently staffing and maintaining resource supplies to be available for all residents whether all residents need them or not.

As an immediate follow-up to arriving at these conclusions, McGregor retained the Center for Applied Research, the research affiliate of LeadingAge, the national affinity group for not-for-profit residential care providers. We awarded the Center with a grant to develop a taxonomy of affordable senior housing providers who excelled at incorporating the needs and preferences of their senior residents into their programs. These exceptional organizations then served as role models for other providers. The model known as "affordable senior housing with services" caught on as an innovative alternative for some low-income populations requiring a nursing home level of care. It contributed to an even more widespread nascent healthcare movement at the time known as "person-centered care."

> **As a DM, I discovered that creating understanding by bringing scholars and providers together can lead to practice innovation.**

Global Aging Network Applied Research Forum

I obviously left the DM Program with a healthy reverence for the value of research to practitioners. Shortly after I graduated in 2006, LeadingAge invited me to join the board of their international affiliate, the International Association of Homes and Service for Aging (IAHSA). Two realizations struck me almost immediately. First, Americans had (and still have) a lot to learn about aging and caring for seniors from other countries. The U.S. is one of only two of at least 40 countries regularly represented at IAHSA conferences that does not provide universal healthcare, the other being Turkey. Universal healthcare typically shields providers from the administrative and political headaches that continuously complicate the lives of U.S. providers dealing with our convoluted system of paying for healthcare, especially for seniors. Technical, architectural, and social innovations outside the U.S. manifest these differences. As a result, Americans are never included among the "cool kids" at IAHSA conferences. Unfortunately, non-American attendees have nothing to learn from us.

Second, international research was not integrated into IAHSA's proceedings as LeadingAge has always attempted domestically, making it difficult for IAHSA's (particularly American) members to learn from each other.

For these reasons, I persuaded our Board to join with our friends at the Benjamin Rose Institute in funding the IAHSA Applied Research Forum. Two internationally known researchers in aging assisted us: Dr. Robyn Stone, SVP of Research at LeadingAge and now the Co-Director of the Leading Age Long-Term Services and Supports (LTSS) Center at UMass Boston (with whom I had worked closely in syndicating the affordable senior housing with services model); and Dr. Julienne Meyer, Professor of Nursing: Care for Older People at City University of London. Dr. Stone and Dr. Meyer convened a network of researchers initially from the U.S., Canada, the UK, and Australia to identify and invite colleagues based outside the U.S. to present their research at IAHSA's biennial conference. This network has since expanded and diversified considerably.

We organized a "preconference" dedicated entirely to research on the day before the main conference started at which academic researchers came together. The specific areas of interest to practitioners were cultural competency, dementia care, housing with services, technology, wellness, and workforce. The agenda included academic presentations followed by discussion panels. The purpose of these discussions was to identify practical questions arising from real world problems that the academic presentations might enlighten or address.

The first forum took place at the 2008 IAHSA conference in Malta. Heavy attendance from the outset immediately confirmed that access to research was an unmet need, and the forums quickly became self-supporting. IAHSA has sponsored subsequent forums in London, Shanghai, Amsterdam, Melbourne, and Lyon, France. A design showcase where architects can display posters of distinctive new projects has emerged as a separate highlight of the conferences. IAHSA, which has changed their name to the "Global Aging Network," will continue to feature "Applied Research Forums" at their future conferences.

I believe that, in addition to conceiving and funding the first of these conferences, perhaps my more enduring contribution was to awaken my fellow practitioners in the Global Aging Network to their inherent, unmet appetite for research. Practitioners in our industry frequently use the term "evidence-based" to validate new practices to funders and boards of directors without understanding either the origins or the legitimacy of the "evidence." The opacity of academic papers discourages their study and application by those not schooled with a facility for research. As a DM, I discovered that creating understanding by bringing scholars and providers together can lead to practice innovation.

Conclusion

As I contemplate retirement at the end of this year, I am fortunate to have worked in the field of aging for nearly 20 years at a very transformative time. McGregor has grown considerably. Staff now numbering more than 500 care for nearly 1,000 primarily low-income seniors every day across a wide variety of care settings. Since we started making grants in 2002 to not-for-profit providers of services and resources to seniors in Cuyahoga County, awards now total more than $15 million. Current and prospective owner/operators of senior housing no longer regard the "with services" model to enable seniors to age in place at home as innovative, but the standard. In addition, advancements in senior care outside the U.S. reveal that sharing research — particularly in the area of technology — can make a significant impact.

I attribute the extent to which I may have contributed to this progress entirely to the DM program. To reassess one's life experience by considering it in the creation of applied knowledge is a remarkable privilege. Enabling access to research by learning its tools and procedures is important for three reasons. First, of course, is the ability to understand problems by breaking them down to their component phenomena in a deliberate, structured manner. Second, is the knowledge gained from building and testing theory from an analysis of these phenomena? Third, and perhaps most important, however, is the new breadth of interest and curiosity that DM students gain from their experience with research. One might ask, what is the critical path to the genesis of a new idea? Surely, the key ingredient is curiosity, which is why the curiosity one cultivates in the DM program is so ultimately rewarding to our careers and our lives.

Keywords
Wellness, Caring, Senior Living, Curiosity

About the Author: R. Robertson Hilton, DM

Dr. Hilton is the President and CEO of The McGregor Foundation, a not-for-profit direct provider and benefactor of residential care, housing and home care to older adults in greater Cleveland. Dr. Hilton received a B.A. in American Studies and Architecture from Wesleyan University in Middletown, Connecticut. He holds an MBA in International Finance from the University of Chicago. Dr. Hilton also received the degree of Doctor of Management from the Weatherhead School of Management at Case Western Reserve University, where his final research project was entitled "Strangers In the Commons: Understanding and Measuring Successful Aging for Low-Income Seniors in Affordable Housing."

Dr. Hilton served as Chairman of the Board of Directors of the International Association of Homes and Services for Aging (IAHSA) in 2012–13. He also serves as a Director of The Evergreen Cooperative Corporation and Green City Growers of Cleveland. Dr. Hilton served previously on the boards of the American Association of Service Coordinators and Grant makers In Aging, which recently named him as honorary life director.

Magdy Amin

The lock-step curriculum of the DM program allows students to explore, discover, and then research their initial impressions through rigorous research methodologies.

Social Change

This is the story of my experience with the Doctor of Management (DM) program. The story started and continued with a positive personal change. I came to the United States in 2005. At that time, a friend of mine told me about the school where he had learned about "appreciative inquiry." We had admired the idea of looking on the positive side of a situation and how to build upon the good side of things in a given situation. Then, in 2005, knowing that I would come to live in Cleveland, this friend told me about Case Western Reserve University (CWRU) and the Weatherhead School of Management, where he had first learned about "appreciative inquiry." For me, it was a big surprise. I opened the website of this university/school to find another surprise: I found that there was a doctoral program for those who had earned a master's degree and had extensive experience in fieldwork. I already had my master's degree in education and much experience with nonprofits and their contributions to education and development in rural and remote areas in Egypt. I completed and sent my application to the managing director, Sue Nartker.

Sue welcomed me, and I found myself in the 2009 cohort of the DM program. My problem of practice were factors that affect the performance of nonprofits in their contribution of education and development. At that time, I faced some difficulties. The first was that I knew a lot about the nonprofits in Egypt, but not about the nonprofits in the United States. The second was about my experience. My experience represented an obstacle, as I found myself tending to talk and write about this experience more than being able to translate it and focus it into research inquiries. It was difficult to be transformed from a field worker to a researcher who asks questions and looks for answers more than being an expert who knows the answers.

I left the DM program and, on the advice of the director of the DM Program, Bo Carlsson, continued to pursue studies in the field of nonprofits. I followed that advice and joined the Mandel Center for Nonprofit Organizations to obtain my Master's degree in Nonprofit Organizations (MNO) in May 2013. Thus, I succeeded in forming a clearer idea about nonprofits in the United States while deepening my perspective about my potential research topic areas that I had started with the DM Program.

During the coursework of the MNO, and before reaching the last courses required to fulfill the program credit hours, the administrators closed the MNO program. There were seven students remaining, therefore, the program asked each one of us to choose some courses within CWRU that would accomplish the required credit hours. I chose three courses; one of them was about leadership. It was a creative course, full of activities and personal assessments that would enable each student to recognize his/her type of leadership. Dr. Tony Lingham was the instructor of this class. He was an associate professor in the Department of Organizational Behavior at the Weatherhead School.

I was fortunate to meet Dr. Lingham during this course. At that time, we discussed my topic of the DM program. It was an opportunity to focus on my topic and the discussion better clarified my understanding and deepened the point that collaboration as one of the factors that may affect the performance of nonprofits.

After obtaining the master's degree at CWRU, I applied again to the DM program. I continued my work and went to the field with questions rather than perspectives. When I was asking my study participants, they used to say, "But you know the answers." My response was "Actually, I don't know, and I want to know your responses." The surprise was that I really did not know the answers. The answers of the participants were opening new horizons and adding many perspectives, which were always beyond my knowledge. They knew the truth. However, the truth was disaggregated among them. Then, I discovered my role, to collect all the mosaics of truth inherent in each one of them and discover the factors that may affect the performance of nonprofits. This was a point of personal change: to discover relationships between the factors within the responses of the participants, relationships that may lead to a theory based on data, which is more powerful than perspective based on an impression or a single situation of experience.

I had several discussions with Dr. Lingham about the data. It was a time of much creativity and support from talented faculty. Finally, I formulated the findings and discovered that the performance in nonprofits is affected by commitment of nonprofits, collaboration among nonprofits, and community participation.

The paper was submitted to Academy of Management (AOM) and was accepted in August 2015. During the time of composing a quantitative paper, I had the chance to work with Dr. Kalle Lyytinen, the Faculty Director of the DM Programs. He was my method advisor for the quantitative paper. Here was another step of learning about how to put my findings/ hypotheses under the light of measurement. The quantitative work confirmed my earlier findings, and this was very revealing and satisfying to me. The lock-step curriculum of the DM program allows students to explore, discover, and then research their initial impressions through rigorous research methodologies.

The quantitative paper was done, submitted, and accepted for the Association for Research on Nonprofit Organizations and Voluntary Action (ARNOVA) conference of November 2016. ARNOVA, such as AOM, was an opportunity to learn and interact with researchers with the same interest in management and social work; however, ARNOVA had its particular interest in the field of nonprofits. During my work on the factors that affect the performance of nonprofits, I was asking myself the following questions:

- What comes after performance?
- What comes after helping nonprofits to capture the factors that enable them to realize a good performance?

The answer was the performance that would help lead to the realization of social change. In other words, the performance would affect change in people and the community. This discovery put me in the situation to return to the DM program to work on this point moreover. I wanted to learn more about what impacts and influences social change in contemporary business and society. I was about to return in August 2017, but a unfortunate event happened. One of my influential figures in my life passed away. He was a priest, a Jesuit monk called Fr. Mounir. Fr. Mounir gave his life to serve youth in remote and deprived areas in Egypt. He was working to serve them and call them to serve others.

When I heard of his passing, I immediately insisted on writing a book about him. For me, Fr. Mounir was an agent of social change. I took two years to work on this book. I used all that I learned in the DM Program to work on the book. For instance, I listened to the priest participants of Fr. Mounir's youth group and put their conversation in transcripts. Within the transcripts, I worked on extracting the codes and build a map of codes. Within the codes, I reached the categories, then the concepts and sub-concepts. It was an attempt to come close to a person to see how he lived his faith and vocation. It was an attempt to explore the achievements of this particular journey of such a person.

The step of writing has been done and I already have started the steps of printing and publishing. The first version will be in Arabic, but it will be translated into English. This book will help to elucidate the stories and events that explain the mission of Fr. Mounir. The book will be entitled *Fr. Mounir: A Call and Dedication of Change*. However, I still would like to continue working on the topic of social change. I would like to explore the grounded theory inherent in our reality that may lead the performance that would realize personal and social change; the performance that may help us to be better and get our reality to be positive and supportive. I am preparing to work on other figures who are also assumed "Agents of Social Change." In working on the above referenced book, I used all that I have learned in the of DM program. The clusters of work could represent an introduction to explore the different elements of "Social Change." In other words, to explore the elements and discover how to apply them in the field. This allows these ideas to be brought forward with practical implications to both the fields of education and development.

Keywords

Transformation, Instructor Roles, Participant Roles, Social Change, Grounded Theory

About the Author: Magdy Amin, DM
Dr. Amin worked for more than 20 years in education and development in Egypt. He started this work with a nonprofit organization with 37 schools in Upper Egypt. This work was an opportunity to discover how to combine education with development. Dr. Amin now works as an education and development consultant in the field of training, capacity building, monitoring and evaluation, and institutional and technical assistance. He has been working with non-profits in Egypt on how to collaborate to realize more impact in the areas of their work. Dr. Amin's work on social change has resulted in a book on a priest who dared to be an "Agent of Social Change."

"The DM programs were built on a strong foundation. The directors of the DM programs lead an orchestra of talented alumni, students, faculty and staff who work together to create a symphony of remarkable accomplishments."

Kalle Lyytinen

Setting the Stage

The DM Programs Directors

John D. Aram

I am privileged to have worked closely with the EDM faculty members. Each brought perspective, expertise, and commitment to our students as well as to the program's design and its success. Without exception, their abilities as scholars and their passion and compassion as teachers were extraordinary.

Executive Doctor of Management Program at Weatherhead: Program Origin and Early Years

Context and Early History

The story of executive doctoral education at Case Western Reserve University cannot be told without recognizing the leadership of Scott S. Cowen, Dean of the Weatherhead School between 1984 and 1998. By the late 1980s, Scott wanted to launch the School to greater national and international visibility and he sought to elevate the School's ranking among business schools. Energetic, ambitious in a positive sense, and innovative by nature, Scott wanted to concentrate the advancement of the School along a number of avenues, and he perceived that executive education was ripe for innovation.

At the time, approximately 80,000 individuals received either an MBA or Executive MBA degree every year from U.S. business schools. Scott observed that there were no academically rigorous, applied educational options available for managers to continue developing intellectually, other than a traditional PhD or non-credit advanced management programs. Consequently, in the late 1980s, Scott charged the faculty with exploring the opportunity for a yet-undefined "post-MBA" degree for experienced managers — a degree program beyond the MBA that would address the learning needs of a significant segment of MBA/EMBA graduates, without requiring them to leave their places of employment. He envisioned something equivalent to a "practice doctorate" in management. Undoubtedly, Scott was also seeking additional revenue streams to support his ambitious plans of increasing the School's impact and visibility.

The process of exploring any non-traditional idea activates a wide range of opinions and engages a number of conflicting interests. At the time, I chaired the Department of Marketing and Policy Studies (MAPS), recently formed by combining faculties of Marketing, Management Policy, and Human Resources/Labor Relations. MAPS consisted of approximately eighteen faculty members, including Drs. Jagdip Singh, Paul Salipante, and Mohan Reddy. Three PhD programs were located in the School — long-standing cohort programs in departments of Organizational Behavior (OB) and Operations Research (OR), as well as a small, struggling PhD program in the MAPS Department with concentrations spread over the department's three academic divisions.

I was dubious, at best, about Scott's idea of an applied doctorate at the School. I saw a new doctoral program as a likely diversion of time and resources away from the need to strengthen the existing MAPS PhD program. MAPS had successfully recruited a number of talented, well-trained, freshly minted PhDs whose career interests were tied to advising traditional doctoral students. Scott and I had a relationship of mutual respect (I had served as his Associate Dean for the early years of his deanship). In a counterintuitive step, he asked me, a vocal skeptic, to chair the faculty committee that would evaluate the new doctorate and make recommendations to the Weatherhead faculty.

Thus formed, the faculty committee began to consider whether a market for an executive doctorate in management could be identified and a suitable educational product could be outlined. We were fortunate to enlist the assistance of a talented new faculty member in Marketing, Dr. Jagdip Singh, to design, administer, and analyze a market study to answer this question. We obtained the cooperation of the Association to Advance Collegiate Schools of Business (AACSB) to generate a random, stratified sample of MBA/EMBA graduates of business schools, weighting the sample toward individuals who would at the time be in the 30–50 year old age range. The survey questionnaire was designed as a series of scales asking respondents to locate themselves between two extremes, such as global to domestic or discipline-oriented to interdisciplinary.

I recall that about 13% of the sample population identified precisely with the qualities of the program that we had in mind (global, interdisciplinary, etc.). Extrapolating to the huge number of MBA/EMBA graduates in general, this result indicated a substantial potential market, and it gave the School a green light to plan a program. At this point, I opted out of my responsibilities at the School to assume a teaching appointment in Madrid, taking an 18-month leave of absence. Dr. Paul Salipante assumed the role of committee chair.

Scott continued to push the program concept with the faculty, recognizing that a major obstacle was the title of the proposed degree. A number of faculty members, mostly affiliated with the PhD programs in OB and OR, objected to using the PhD designation for a non-traditional, practice-oriented doctoral program. In the end, Scott surveyed the faculty in a written questionnaire, asking whether faculty members would support a new doctoral degree if it were titled an Executive Doctor in Management (EDM).

Owing to the quality of the participants, faculty work in the program often was as energizing and rewarding as any other teaching experiences, or more so.

The results of that survey showed approval, even if it may have been reluctant approval. When I returned from my leave, Scott asked me to continue to lead the planning committee and to be the first director of the new program, which at the time was envisioned as a 36 credit hour program. I was no longer MAPS Department chair and the notion of playing a role in an innovative program of executive education at the doctoral level with a global focus appealed to me. Like most others, I found Scott's personal charm and strategic vision irresistible. I signed on.

Detailed planning led to a series of curricular decisions that increased the credit hour requirements of the program. From a 36 credit hour program, it became a 42 credit hour program and then it became a 48 credit hour program. In order to meet the requirements of the Ohio Board of Regents, it became a 54 credit hour program. The Board of Regents also specified a prior master's degree of at least 36 credit hours, resulting in a final requirement for 90 total graduate credit hours. Scott used his extraordinary skills of persuasion to usher the program through the University administration and the CWRU Faculty Senate, and I pitched the program to the Board of Regents review committee.

The faculty committee had designed an innovative program embracing a broad concept of management. Committee members subscribed to the belief that many MBA/EMBA graduates who had achieved senior positions in their areas of expertise would welcome a program to broaden their horizons, to study fresh perspectives and ideas, and to conduct applied research. In this regard, we looked to the liberal arts, especially the social sciences, and designed nontraditional management topics, such as collective action, culture and world politics, the social construction of technology, technological systems, adult competency development, environmental law and policy, among other courses.

In order to give the program geographical appeal, we planned to draw upon emerging digital technology to include a distance-learning component, deciding on a format of periodic residencies with online communications between residencies. The program design called for six on-campus visits per semester. We also sought a configuration of program participants to reflect as great personal and professional diversity as the pool of qualified applicants would allow.

Marketing and Administrative Support

Once approved, we marketed the new program to alumni of the Weatherhead MBA programs; several alumni applied and were accepted in the inaugural program class. In addition, consistent with our aspirations to establish a national and international reputation, we purchased advertisements in *The Wall Street Journal* and *The Economist*, and that visibility worked well for the program. While quite expensive, these media outlets put the program on the executive education map in both the U.S. and overseas and consistently generated highly qualified applicants. After several years, Dr. John Palmer Smith, faculty member in the Mandel School of Applied Social Sciences (SASS), helped us to secure a multi-year grant from the Packard Foundation to support scholarships for students in the nonprofit sector.

Until we actually had tuition-paying students in the program, I needed to beg and borrow administrative and secretarial support around the School. Administrative staff in MAPS were unavailable for an additional workload, so Dr. Scott Cowen asked Richard Osborne, Director of the Center for Management Development and Research, to make staff time temporarily available in that office for program mailings, correspondence, etc. In a stroke of good fortune, Richard asked (directed) Sue Nartker to assist my efforts.

Sue opened a new world for me of what administrative support could mean. She was proficient and efficient while being friendly and always service oriented. She thought ahead and could anticipate needs, and most importantly, she could solve administrative bottlenecks and other problems. Due to prior training with computers, Sue was competent with technology, and her welcoming and responsive style on the phone and in person was (and is) unparalleled. Earlier studies and experience in fashion merchandising gave her a flair for designing promotional materials as well as for paying close attention to participants' total program experiences. I enjoyed first-class administrative support. The continuing presence of Sue and Marilyn Chorman (who later joined the program staff from the Center for Management Development and Research) has been a positive legacy.

In my view, the key to the quality of our program, and really to any academic program, is what happens in the classroom. Sue and Marilyn intuitively understood this and they did everything possible to support students' learning experiences.

Program Underway

Consistent with my view of educational quality, I felt it imperative that the program consistently deliver a superior educational experience. To this end, I was sensitive to how the various seminars were working out. By student and faculty reports, some were going fabulously; others needed early course corrections. After several iterations of faculty, we were able to recruit Richard Boyatzis and Jagdip Singh to teach critically important courses in their fields. In fairly short order, the early program teaching faculty consisted of Drs. Mohan Reddy, Paul Salipante, Bo Carlsson, Dick Boland, Richard Boyatzis, Jagdip Singh, Dennis Young, myself, and Wendy Wagner, JD, from the Law School.

Faculty adopted several classroom innovations. For example, Paul, Mohan, and I were teaching the first year students in the first semester of the program. We worked to coordinate not only our reading material, but also the timing of our assignments. In addition, I look back favorably on our use of post-residency "reflection papers" as a useful teaching innovation. By Tuesday of the week following a residency, each student and each of the three faculty members wrote a short, substantive, non-graded reflection on their most important conclusions from the residency — connecting, critiquing, integrating, and reacting to the assigned material and the discussions across all three seminars. Not only did I find this assignment productive for myself, I also profited greatly from reading others' thoughtful papers.

Another unusual procedure was end-of-first-year student evaluations. At the conclusion of each spring term, I would talk with each of the faculty who had taught the first year EDM students to obtain feedback about each student, particularly with an eye to that student's development. Then, I wrote summary letters to each student over the summer conveying the positive comments that had come out of these discussions and identifying development tasks for the student's focus in the coming year. In retrospect, I am not sure those letters made much difference to the students, but at least they made me feel like I was doing something that might benefit the students.

After several years, Mohan, who was teaching the Collective Action seminar, needed to devote his time to other projects. This created a huge gap in the teaching faculty. Learning that the Political Science Department at CWRU had just hired a new PhD from U.C. Berkeley in International Relations, Dr. Eileen Doherty, I asked to meet with her and the chairman of her department, first to get acquainted, and second to see if the EDM program could purchase part of her salary to teach Culture and World Politics, switching me to the Collective Action course. I was eager to have a true political scientist teaching that course and I felt comfortable switching to the collective action seminar. Eileen responded enthusiastically to the idea of joining our faculty and today she continues to inspire program students with her knowledge, thoughtfulness, and openness. Eileen also wholeheartedly participated in thought-piece summaries following each residency in the first semester.

Life happens, and other faculty members needed to move on for various reasons. Overtime, we were fortunate to add Peter Gerhart, JD (Law School) and Dr. Jeff Longhofer (School of Applied Social Sciences) to our regular teaching faculty. I was also happy to enlist Tom Anderson,

JD, a Fellow in the Center for Professional Ethics at CWRU, to teach a third-year course in Culture in the Arts. A few years later, Tom regularly taught Social Ethics: Contemporary Issues, in the third program year. The number of faculty within Weatherhead and in the wider University who taught elective seminars and served as guest speakers or research supervisors are too many to mention individually, but they were indispensable to the program. Students and faculty also enjoyed seminars with prestigious outside speakers, such as Dr. Fareed Zakaria, Dr. Elinor Ostrom and Dr. Carl Safina along with a wide range of scholars and practitioners.

I am privileged to have worked closely with the EDM faculty members. Each brought perspective, expertise, and commitment to our students as well as to the program's design and its success. Without exception, their abilities as scholars and their passion and compassion as teachers were extraordinary.

Outcomes

I wish time and space would allow me to comment about EDM students that I admitted to the program, knew as student participants, and worked with in the classroom. I can say that generally the level of commitment to learning, dedication to preparation, and quality of thinking of EDM students during my watch surpassed expectations. Owing to the quality of the participants, faculty work in the program often was as energizing and rewarding as any other teaching experiences, or more so. Working on intellectual tasks with experienced, committed, reflective, and well-prepared adult learners in an environment of co-learning was wonderfully gratifying.

It is highly satisfying for me to hear program alumni offer testimonials about the program's transformative impact on their lives and their careers. Not infrequently, I am impressed to learn of the depth and extent of graduates' attributions to the program. It is also a source of personal satisfaction to follow the production of books, papers, presentations and other professional contributions by alumni. I am deeply grateful to our alumni for their contributions, both during and after the program.

As I reached retirement age, I was aware of a number of things I wanted to do in my senior years, so I took the opportunity to make an exit and I resigned as a CWRU faculty member to let others pick up the reins.

In closing, let me recognize that teaching is a helping profession. If, as an administrator or a teacher, I have been instrumental in EDM students' growth and development, I feel my professional life is justified. I am profoundly grateful to Dr. Scott Cowen, the EDM alumni, the faculty, and our administrative staff for the opportunity to have shared a most gratifying personal journey.

Key words
Executive Doctoral Education, Practice Based Doctorate, Interdisciplinary, Innovation

About the Author: John D. Aram, PhD
Dr. Aram was a faculty member at the Weatherhead School of Management at Case Western Reserve University for nearly forty years, fulfilling various academic and administrative roles as professor of organizational behavior and later, of management policy. His academic work focused on organizational behavior, business and public policy, and the integration of management theory and practice. Between 1995 and 2005, he serves as Director of the Doctor of Management (DM\EDM) program at Weatherhead. He finished his career as professor and associate dean in the Graduate School of Arts and Social Sciences at Lesley University in Cambridge, MA.

His wife and he retired in 2007 in Boston, MA. Since then, they have divided their time between Boston and Seville, Spain, where their daughter is professor of early modern European history at Pablo de Olavide University. In addition, their son and his family live in Chappaqua, NY, and he is CEO of a privately held firm.

In Boston, as in Cleveland, Dr. Aram has worked with a variety of civic, community, and political organizations. For about eight years, he has served as an intake volunteer at the American Civil Liberties Union of Massachusetts. He also regularly participates in the Evergreen Program at Boston University, a program in which seniors attend courses on an audit basis.

Bo Carlsson

It would be an integration of theory and practice and rigorous research with a practitioner-scholar rather than academic focus. Nothing like that had been done before; this was unique and groundbreaking.

Personal Reflections on the DM Program

Planning for the Program

The idea of creating a new type of doctoral program for practicing executives was exciting to me from the start. My background of education and research at Harvard, Stanford, and MIT and nearly 14 years of work at the Industrial Institute for Economic and Social Research in Stockholm, Sweden, had given me a broad perspective on research that spans disciplinary boundaries — economics, management, engineering, economic history and geography. In my own research I had always found it regrettable, for example, that macroeconomics, microeconomics, and management had evolved into separate disciplines without much boundary-spanning research and without much interest in practical application.

I came to CWRU in 1984 to chair the Department of Economics. In the early 1990s, the Economics Department moved from the College of Arts and Sciences into the Weatherhead School of Management. At that time, there had already been discussion for a few years about developing new post-MBA programs. I welcomed the opportunity to work with people in management in designing the new program, which eventually became the Executive Doctor of Management (EDM) program.

When I was asked to join the planning team, the basic features had already been agreed upon: a doctorate in professional management designed for top-level executives who hold an advanced degree in their field and who would value and benefit from interdisciplinary experience. It would be an integration of theory and practice and rigorous research with a practitioner-scholar rather than academic focus. Nothing like that had been done before; this was unique and groundbreaking. What remained was to design the content and structure of the program.

The program team was handpicked to include leading scholars in several disciplines — people with tenure and broad experience, who were willing and able to take a broad interdisciplinary view, and who were not forced by the tenure clock to produce more publications in their particular discipline. It was clear from the beginning that we needed to create an entirely new type of program. In order to create value for organizational leaders with many years of experience and practice in a management field, we needed to create courses beyond the traditional MBA curriculum. People who are at an inflection point in their careers need to decide whether to advance to the next level (often requiring new skills) or consider other career options beyond their previous experience.

As our discussions evolved, it became increasingly clear that the new program would need to:

1. Provide state-of-the art knowledge in a rapidly changing global environment. This would require new courses with both interdisciplinary and integrative content; standard courses in conventional management sub-disciplines would not be sufficient; and

2. Build on each student's experience and complement it with practical and rigorous research skills; the research questions would be derived from problems of practice identified by the students, not by standard academic theory.

We recognized that the knowledge basis of the traditional MBA deals primarily with management practices internal to the firm, while post-MBA education should deal with social, economic, and political processes that have an impact on the firm but are not directly under management control. Issues and problems of interest in the program would be inherently multi-disciplinary and would often require a global perspective. As a result, new courses had to be developed – a welcome challenge for all of us. In my case, it provided an opportunity to study topics that had interested me for a long time and to integrate them with my own research. Exploring such topics with experienced professionals with a wide variety of backgrounds and perspectives was exciting.

The course that I developed for the program (Business as a Dynamic System: The Evolution of Organizational Structure) gave me an opportunity to explore topics concerning the evolution of modern industrial enterprise in both historical and international perspective, as well as the role of culture and finance as determinants of business organization, ownership, and governance. One part of the course dealt with the evolution of regional innovation systems and industry clusters. The second part focused on the role of entrepreneurship as well as public policy in that process. A third segment focused on some of the main drivers of organizational and structural change in the economy in the last few decades: digitization, the Internet, and globalization. How do these drivers influence the boundaries of firms, corporate strategy, and organization?

What we came up with was a new kind of practitioner-oriented PhD that is focused on integrating theory and practice and that is not discipline-based but builds on a foundation of systems thinking, sustainability, and design: the PhD in Management: Designing Sustainable Systems.

The course was originally placed in the second semester of the first year and was designed to help students think about the evolution of business systems in various contexts as they framed their own research in a multi-disciplinary framework. Sometimes the problem of practice based on the students' own management experience falls neatly into the domain of a particular sub-discipline. However, in the DM program, most of the time it does not, at least in my own experience as an advisor in the program. The relevant domain may be in the intersection between several sub-disciplines, which means a significant challenge for the student but also for the academic advisor whose expertise is typically in only a narrow sub-discipline. The students are asked to find out and summarize what is written about the problem and then articulate a research question. The true challenge lies in framing the research question.

In a discipline-based doctoral program, the research questions typically fall within well-defined disciplinary boundaries. However, in a truly cross-disciplinary program the research domain is much broader and less well defined. The challenge for the advisor is to determine where his or her expertise can help and then to learn, along with the student, where to seek new knowledge and make sense of it. It is truly a journey of discovery — exciting!

The program as a whole is designed to help students in the process of framing and articulating their research questions. The academic advisor is the coach, while the student becomes the real expert on the topic at hand. After all, that is the true meaning of a doctoral education.

How has the program evolved over the years?
The overall aims of EDM inquiry, which evolved into the Doctor of Management (DM) program during my tenure as director, have remained constant:

1) to develop capabilities for creating new knowledge and insights into problems of practice using a coherent framework and language that bridges theory and practice through diverse methodologies; and

2) through the process of building capabilities for knowledge creation, to provide transformative experiences for thoughtful practitioners to foster a community of practitioner-scholars who are engaged in life-long scholarship and who actively lead the practitioner and academic discourse on policy, practice and public issues of management.

The main features of the program have remained largely the same:

- Transdisciplinary curriculum (including Humanities and Social Sciences): Management in a broad sense
- Integrative inquiry courses
- Both qualitative and quantitative research methods required
- Heavy research emphasis: the "Scholarly Practitioner"
- Broad global perspective and participation
- Transformational, globally oriented, cross-disciplinary research-intensive program for organizational leaders.

The basic structure of the program has remained the same: a 3-year, residency-based program. However, the number, duration, and scheduling of residencies and how best to use communication technology were discussed from time to time, as was the possibility of locating residencies elsewhere in the world. The balance between integrative (interdisciplinary) and research methods courses has shifted slightly over the years toward more research methods courses. The inquiry methods have also shifted toward more emphasis on quantitative research and introduction of mixed methods research (using both qualitative and quantitative analysis).

In the early years of the program students were required to write reflection papers following each residency in which they were asked to integrate and reflect on the learnings from each seminar as well as on the residency as a whole. In addition, in the beginning each student was required to complete an Applied Research Project (ARP) based on his or her portfolio papers (summarizing the takeaways from each year) and an integrative summary — essentially similar to a doctoral dissertation. Later the degree requirement was changed to a sequence of papers (a conceptual paper in year 1, a qualitative research paper in year 2, a quantitative research paper and an integrative paper in year 3).

Issues in running the program

The greatest challenge in running the program soon after I became Faculty Director was that for a couple of years we had a dean who essentially wanted to eliminate the program. Fortunately, an external evaluation ("Fresh Look") committee provided valuable recommendations to continue and improve the program.

A perennial challenge in running the program was the need to increase the number and engagement of faculty teaching and advising in the program. This was driven by the need to find suitable advisors for student research, as well as the desirability of developing new courses and of staffing courses when faculty were on leave or made other commitments. The high expectations of our students with respect to faculty commitment of time and effort and the transdisciplinary nature of student research, combined with the School's need to staff other programs and the pressure on non-tenured faculty to publish within their own disciplines to qualify for tenure significantly reduced the number of potentially available faculty. One-way in which we tried to expose more faculty to the DM program and vice versa was through a set of courses entitled Frontiers in Management. These courses were intended to expose students to leading researchers in various management-related domains, to identify some of the main issues at the research frontier and learn about how to frame research questions and pursue research in those domains, as well as to discuss the practical and policy implications of the findings. Practical issues made it necessary to abandon the effort after a couple of years.

As the quantitative research in the program expanded, there was a need to find more research methods teachers and advisors. Several faculty members at Weatherhead as well as the Law School, the College of Arts and Sciences, and the School of Medicine took up the challenge. We also found that many of our recent graduates were willing and able to provide valuable assistance.

The most fundamental change toward the end of my tenure as Faculty Director was the addition of the PhD option (Designing Sustainable Systems). Three motivations drove this initiative: 1) to meet the desire of some applicants and current students to conduct more advanced inquiry than the three-year DM Program could support; 2) to respond to shifting trends in the Academy for enhanced focus on scholarship that bridges theory and practice; and 3) to solidify our position as the leading innovator in doctoral programs for practitioner-scholars.

We recognized, somewhat to our surprise, that even though the DM program was designed for practicing executives, many of our graduates found themselves highly qualified for and attracted to academic pursuits, either in part-time academic teaching while pursuing practitioner careers or as a full-time career. Equipped with rigorous research skills, often superior to those of graduates of traditional PhD programs (because of the DM requirement of applying both qualitative and quantitative research methods), and with experience of multidisciplinary and integrative research, an increasing number of DM graduates discovered opportunities that we had not foreseen when we originally designed the program. Given the poor name recognition of the DM degree in academia, where the PhD is the expected (and better understood) standard, we wanted to make it easier for our graduates to fill this market need.

In our deliberations about adding the PhD option, several issues and concerns came up. The DM program was clearly a success. We did not want to diminish its value; rather, we wanted to build on its success. Fifteen years after the launch of the DM program, competing programs were beginning to emerge, validating the DM concept but also challenging us to maintain leadership as the premier professional (post-MBA) management program in the world. What we came up with was a new kind of practitioner-oriented PhD that is focused on integrating theory and practice and that is not discipline-based but builds on a foundation of systems thinking, sustainability, and design: the PhD in Management: Designing Sustainable Systems. Our expectation was that this innovation would increase penetration into academia, influencing the academic curriculum in the direction of integrating theory and practice, as well as enhancing the level of practitioner scholarship more generally.

Concluding Comments

My DM journey has been stimulating, challenging, and enriching all along. I have enjoyed interacting with students with varying backgrounds and experience from around the world. In working with them on novel and interesting topics, I could not help but learn. Discussing ideas with them and with highly innovative, insightful and knowledgeable colleagues and world-class scholars in order to create a stimulating learning environment for a unique community of scholars has been truly enriching. I am a better scholar, human being, and global citizen as a result.

Keywords
Transformational, Globally Oriented, Cross-disciplinary Research-intensive, Integrative Inquiry Courses

About the Author: Bo Carlsson, PhD
Dr. Carlsson is Professor of Economics (Emeritus) and former Director of the Doctor of Management Program and Associate Dean for Research and Graduate Programs at the Weatherhead School of Management. From 1972 to 1984, he was Research Associate and Associate Director of the Institute for Industrial Economics (IFN) in Stockholm, Sweden. He

has had visiting appointments at the University of Washington, Massachusetts Institute of Technology (M.I.T.), Chalmers University of Technology, and the University of Paris and currently holds an appointment as a Research Affiliate at the Center for Innovation, Research, and Competence in the Learning Economy (CIRCLE) at Lund University in Sweden.

Dr. Carlsson has published over 20 books and numerous articles in industrial economics, small business and entrepreneurship, technological change, innovation systems and innovation policy. He has pioneered in Industrial Dynamics — a new field in economics, which he initiated in 1985. His current research focuses on entrepreneurial systems in the life sciences in Sweden and Ohio and on the Experimentally Organized Economy.

Dr. Carlsson has served on several government commissions in Sweden and been a consultant to the World Bank, the Swedish Agency for Innovation Systems, VINNOVA, the Norwegian Research Council, the Academy of Finland, and private industry. In 1984–86, he was President of the European Association for Research in Industrial Economics. He was chair of the International Scientific Advisory Board of the Danish Research Unit for Industrial Dynamics (DRUID) 1995–2008. He was a member of the Global Award for Entrepreneurship Research Prize Committee, 2009 – 2014 and it's Chair, 2011–2014. In 2012–14, he was Vice President of the International Joseph A. Schumpeter Society.

Kalle Lyytinen

*When my colleagues ask me about my experience
in leading the DM programs, I always say that
this has been my best experience as an academic
citizen. The program manifests the great idea of
"universitas" — a universal and common search
for knowledge and truth through learning and
argument in the community of inquirers where
scholars and practitioners jointly participate
as equal citizens.*

Executive Doctor of Management Program at Weatherhead: Adolescence and Growth to Maturity

Context

I started managing the DM program in the academic year of 2008–2009. I had just returned from a year sabbatical which included a research stay and teaching in Lausanne, Switzerland and Helsinki, Finland. My knowledge about the DM program before taking the helm was largely hearsay, ad hoc, and haphazard at best. I had learned about this mystic program mainly by its visible appearance in constant frequency when a couple of rooms in the Peter B. Lewis building had something to eat and more mature persons wandered around.

At that time some of my colleagues in the Management Information Decision Sciences department (Drs. Dick Boland and Michel Avital), who taught in the program, were quite busy and they spoke about their experience in vague terms. I had also met Dr. John Aram a few times in 2004–2006 while managing a research grant offered by Cleveland Foundation at the school level. The grant focused on advancing virtual learning environments and promoting digital pedagogy. I remember John applying for a significant amount of money from the grant for the DM program to support digital ways of distributing program content and research outputs by editing and formatting it for digital publication. We did not grant the full requested amount despite John's forceful arguments, but I first got a sense of what the program was about from this interaction. The people in it were passionate about it and their mission. I also learned something about DM research projects in 2005–2006 when I advised a couple of DM students who examined the diffusion

of mobile and other information technologies. I advised them on their thesis work based on the request of Dr. Dick Boland.

My real litmus test with the program came after the sabbatical. I promised to teach a course on scales and measurement theory, which had been left vacant when Dr. Michel Avital moved to Europe. Shortly after that, Dr. Bo Carlsson asked whether I would take the responsibility of leading the whole program. I still do not know exactly why I was selected as a candidate and who would have been the alternative had I turned the offer down. Luckily, I chose to accept the request. The main reason was not really the lure of the program, as I knew little of it. The more rational and practical reason was that I had little reason to decline the request. I had been on the WSOM faculty nearly eight years and knew that at some point I would have to carry some heavier administrative responsibility.

When I accepted the request, I asked Bo why he would not continue as the director. He said that he had successfully implemented the expansion of the program with the addition of the PhD option and had managed to change the program name to DM (rather than the original Executive Doctor of Management or EDM). He thought that it was for others to implement these changes and to seek good ways to integrate and execute the PhD and DM programs. The foundation was also in place. Several significant changes had taken place during Bo's tenure. These included the introduction of both qualitative and quantitative research projects and related articles, as well as the idea of an integrated DM thesis based on a combination of the two research pieces. This practice had already been part of the program requirements for a couple of years by the time I took the leadership responsibility. They, therefore, provided a solid foundation upon which I could start implementing the PhD option.

When I came to the position, I already had significant experience in managing, mentoring and organizing PhD programs both in Europe and at Weatherhead. I had advised or mentored over 30 PhD students, of whom many had had successful academic or industry careers (including managing start-ups). Therefore, the first thing I decided to do was to frame the PhD implementation based on my experience of what works and does not work in doctoral education. At the time I accepted the

leadership position, I was also told that the program could not expand significantly in terms of new course work, number of courses, and course variation within the DM part to ensure a common experience for all students. In line with these constraints, I decided to keep the three first years of the DM and PhD program nearly identical, and include both DM and PhD students in the same cohort during the third year. I also decided that we would not accept students directly to the PhD program, but instead the selection would happen during the second year of the DM program. This would make marketing and admissions management simpler and less risky; it would also offer easier pathways for students to move back and forth between the two options. I also made two significant additions to the method sections of the DM program. First, I made the advanced statistics class a requirement for the PhD students (and optional for the DM students); second, I introduced a mixed methods class to serve as an integrating method class for DM students and the baseline capstone course for PhD students on research design thesis proposal development. These innovations have remained and have been strengthened since 2009–2010 when these decisions were made.

Another major effort was writing administrative guidelines and requirements for the PhD option, getting them approved by the School of Graduate Studies, and developing practical arrangements with the entire faculty to coordinate the student related activities with the School of Graduate Studies. Here the administrative support, insight and diligence of both Sue Nartker and Marilyn Chorman was of enormous help; with their support, all the administrative materials were written in a relatively short period during 2009–2010. I also decided that DM/PhD students would need to follow the same requirements and guidelines that traditional PhD students at Weatherhead follow. We had to establish requirements for building thesis committees, designing comprehensive examinations using an extensive baseline list of readings, and creating expectations of public, carefully orchestrated and rigorous proposal and thesis defenses.

One important challenge was to get a large body of interdisciplinary faculty to agree on the same set of requirements and to follow similar procedures as part of the thesis committee work. Each department and faculty member appeared to have their own idea how this process

should be run. Some claimed that the requirements I set up were too stringent and demanding, while others stated that they were still too lax. Despite these initial complaints, these practices and principles have been largely followed across all PhD processes. In doing this, the program has ensured the unity of the thesis writing process and made sure that the students meet largely similar intellectual and academic requirements as traditional PhD students would do. This was deemed important to ensure the quality and respectability of the new PhD program in the eyes of the faculty — both inside and outside the school. We also received external testimony to this success when Drs. Kim Cameron and Denise Rousseau in their review of the PhD program in 2015 called the program "the only premier program in this arena".

An important final decision in creating the PhD was the decision to run it as part of the cohort model, but without additional course work. To this end, I sequenced the execution of writing a thesis over a period of 15 months (in which I think all PhD theses should be written) and organized the process into multiple steps such as building a commit-tee, preparing for and attending the comprehensive exams, writing and defending the proposal, executing the thesis research, and writing it for the dissertation defense. I also thought that during the fourth year the key focus should be on writing an additional third paper (typically students would have two research articles already written) and writing an additional synthesis paper with an extensive literature review. These were deemed necessary to guarantee adequate scope for the thesis work and to make sure that it was anchored in appropriate academic research traditions. The cohort structure was maintained by organizing the thesis writing around five consecutive workshops (one in summer, two in fall, and two in early spring of the fourth year) where students would have time to present critique and get feedback of their thesis work.

The aim of the workshops was to acquaint students with academic research seminars and help them learn to constructively review academic work. Until that point, the organization of the DM program did not offer space for such activities as 90 percent of the residency time goes to course work and related deliverables. All these principles were implemented for the first time in the 2010–2011 PhD cohort and in each cohort thereafter with small refinements and improvements every year. Sometimes we have had one rotating research seminar group and

sometimes two groups, depending on the size of the cohort. The principle has been that each student should have 45 minutes to present and discuss his or her research project in each residency.

Program Improvement

When I took the helm of the program, it had been operating for approximately 15 years. During this period, many different types of educational arrangements and interventions had been tried. Because of these experiments, the idea of nine interdisciplinary subject area courses and nine research competency and method courses appeared to work well. We also found that the idea that the students need to work through both qualitative and quantitative research inquiry while dealing with the research problem was an excellent practice for advancing student's research skills. Generally, this meant that most students followed a research journey that combined a mixed method research approach with a complementary, open and development focus. Because this all worked well and had the support of both students and faculty, I decided not to change these pillars during my tenure without a very good reason. So far, no such compelling reason has emerged.

> I have learned that the universitas of DM programs is fundamentally about the social bonding and community building that is so essential for the human condition.

The main program development focus during my tenure has been to improve general research quality and rigor of student research outputs. This has meant two things: first, integrating and improving faculty collaborations within and across research method courses; second, introducing additional skills development components to the curriculum such as library resources, software tool use, academic writing skills, improvement of pedagogic skills, how to improve research dissemination and impact on practice, and so on. All these topics have been integrated as part of the courses or as separate independently standing workshops during the residencies. We have also introduced a student research presentation symposia to integrate learning across and within cohorts; these occur twice a year, one in August and another one in January. Another improvement in my tenure has been to establish frequent

and consistent faculty meetings where key issues around pedagogy, course development, student mentoring and program development and marketing are discussed. These have served as important arenas for many of the innovations and improvements mentioned above. These meetings built a strong and shared vision, commitment and values around the program faculty. We have also introduced 'strategy' days where program faculty, students and alumni work on strategic development issues related to program development and marketing. Among other things, these have focused on how to improve the visibility and value of the DM option, how to improve program pedagogy, how to make the program easier to attend by reducing the number of residencies while seeking to maintain the quality.

Outcomes

When I took the helm of the program, it had 47 full time DM students. There were some concerns at that time of the size and viability of the program. Therefore, I have sought to systematically increase the size of the program to a more viable level. This has been also successful, particularly after adding the PhD option in 2010. In the 2016–2017 academic year, the program had nearly 90 students. Since then the overall size has declined as competition has intensified, but we are still well over 60 students and remain one of the largest residency-based high quality programs. As a result, the alumni base has also grown from about 100 (in the first 15 years) to close to 300 (in the subsequent 10 years). The program has produced 83 PhD degrees in the last 9 years and is currently one of the largest degree granting PhD programs in business schools.

Other significant outcomes during this period included the introduction of Engaged Management ReView journal that promotes and distributes practitioner-scholarship research and the Engaged Practitioner Scholars Fellowship (EPS@Case) which advances practice-oriented research and its dissemination. The first has concentrated on publishing and advocating globally high quality engaged management scholarship with innovative genres and engagement models. This is a joint initiative with the Executive DBA Council (EDBAC). The latter aims to build up and sustain a vibrant and supportive engaged management scholarship community among the nearly 300 DM program alumni. Currently over 20 alumni participate in EPS activities.

All of this would not have been possible without the support of excellent and expedient staff and the ideas and commitment of a large group of faculty at Weatherhead, CWRU, and other universities who have devoted their time, energy and wits to teach and mentor a magnificent group of DM programs students. When my colleagues ask me about my experience in leading the DM programs, I always say that this has been my best experience as an academic citizen. The program manifests the great idea of "universitas" — a universal and common search for knowledge and truth through learning and argument in the community of inquirers where scholars and practitioners jointly participate as equal citizens.

The DM programs has also expanded my idea of universitas with novel insights about the inner worlds and behaviors of its citizens, opening windows to the outside, and appreciation of the essential value of social bonding and connectedness with which our journeys tie us. The universitas of DM programs is not just for the leisurely gentlemen of words and wisdom to search eternal truths in their ivory towers. Rather it is to promote intellectual and ethical growth of its members in ways that foster personal maturity, improve the organizations they serve, and make the society and human kind at large better. The universitas of DM programs wants to also look outside the windows of the ivory tower and reach out to learn how discovered knowledge and truths are translated into action and influence. We constantly strive to promote and understand evidence-based management. Finally, I have learned that the universitas of DM programs is fundamentally about the social bonding and community building that is so essential for the human condition. It is in this universitas where "bands of brothers and sisters" must come together, bond and then succeed, because of their shared drive, motivation and accomplishments despite the hardships and challenges they meet during their journey.

Keywords

Academic Administration, Doctoral Education, Interdisciplinary, Pedagogy, Universitas

About the Author: Kalle Lyytinen, PhD

Dr. Lyytinen is the Iris S. Wolstein Professor of Management Design; Chair and Professor, Design and Innovation Department; Faculty Director, Doctor of Management Programs, and CWRU Distinguished University Professor. His research helps define how rapidly changing digital innovations shape organizations. His work helps organizations know how to identify, absorb, manage, implement and be transformed by digital innovations. Dr. Lyytinen's recent projects have focused on engineering practices, open innovation and software development organizations where he studies the adoption and assimilation of new technologies, new forms of collaboration, and ways to determine system requirements. Dr. Lyytinen joined the Weatherhead School of Management faculty in 2001. Since then his teaching interests have focused on digital innovation theory, new business venturing, design theory and methods, research methods and theory. He has an extensive list of over 400 publications in numerous prestigious journals and books and special editions. He is one of the top 5 most cited scholars in the field of information systems.

References

Adelowotan, M. O., & Olaoluniyi, O. (2015). *Significance of Human Capital to Organisational Value Creation*. Paper presented at the 1st Academic Conference of Accounting and Finance, Lagos, Nigeria.

Andelfinger, U. (2002). On the intertwining of social and technical factors in software development projects. In Y. Dittrich, C. Floyd, & R. Klischewski (Eds.), *Social thinking-software practice* (pp. 185–203). Cambridge, MA: MIT Press.

Arthur, W. B. (1990). Positive feedbacks in the economy. *Scientific American, 262*(2), 92–99.

Baron, R. A. (2006). Opportunity recognition as pattern recognition: how entrepreneurs "connect the dots" to identify new business opportunities. *Academy of Management Perspectives, 20*(1), 104–119. doi:10.5465/AMP.2006.19873412

Baron, R. A., & Ensley, M. D. (2006). Opportunity recognition as the detection of meaningful patterns: evidence from comparisons of novice and experienced entrepreneurs. *Management Science, 52*(9), 1331–1344. doi:10.1287/mnsc.1060.0538

Becker, B. E., & Huselid, M. A. (2006). Strategic Human Resources Management: Where Do We Go From Here? *Journal of Management, 32*(6), 898–925. doi:10.1177/0149206306293668

Birkinshaw, J., Bresman, H., & Håkanson, L. (2000). Managing the post-acquisition integration process: how the human integration and task integration processes interact to foster value creation. *Journal of Management Studies, 37*(3).

Boulding, K. E. (1966). The economics of knowledge and the knowledge of economics. *American Economic Review, 56*(2), 1–13.

Boyatzis, R. E. (1998). *Transforming qualitative information.* Thousand Oaks, CA: SAGE Publications.

Brooks Jr., F. P. (1986). *No silver bullet — essence and accidents of software engineering.* Paper presented at the International Federation for Information Processing 10th World Computer Conference, Dublin, Ireland.

Buono, A. F., Bowditch, J. L., & Lewis, J. W. (1985). When cultures collide: the anatomy of a merger. *Human Relations, 38*(5), 477–500. doi:10.1177/001872678503800506

Bureau of Labor Statistics, United States Department of Labor. (2018). Annual layoffs and discharges levels by industry and region, not seasonally adjusted. Retrieved from https://www.bls.gov/news.release/jolts.t19.htm

Cagan, M. (2017). *Inspired: how to create tech products customers love.* Hoboken, NJ: John Wiley & Sons.

Cal. S. B. 826 (2017–2018), Chapter 954 (Cal. Stat. 2018).

Campbell, C. (2019). Emerging technologies in accounting. *CPA IN Perspective, Summer,* 36–39.

Campbell, C., & Fogarty, T. J. (2018). Behind the curve: higher education's efforts to implement advanced information systems. *Journal of Emerging Technologies in Accounting, 15*(2), 77–91. doi:10.2308/jeta-52237

Cardon, M. S., Wincent, J., Singh, J., & Drnovsek, M. (2009). The nature and experience of entrepreneurial passion. *Academy of Management Review, 34*(3), 511–532. doi:10.5465/AMR.2009.40633190

Caruso, P., Dumbacher, D., & Grieves, M. W. (2010). *Product lifecycle management and the quest for sustainable space exploration.* Paper presented at the AIAA SPACE 2010 Conference & Exposition, Anaheim, CA.

Castellanos, S. (2017, March 21). GE's digital replicas, which monitor machines, gain a voice. *The Wall Street Journal.* Retrieved from https://blogs.wsj.com/cio/2017/03/21/ges-digital-replicas-which-monitor-machines-gain-a-voice/

Chandler Jr., A. D. (1990). *Scale and scope: the dynamics of industrial capitalism.* Cambridge, MA: Harvard University Press.

Chen, G., Gully, S. M., & Eden, D. (2001). Validation of a new general self-efficacy scale. *Organizational Research Methods, 4*(1), 62–83. doi:10.1177/109442810141004

Christensen, C. M., & Raynor, M. E. (2003). Why hard-nosed executives should care about management theory. *Harvard Business Review, 81*(9), 66–74.

Coates, J. (2019). *Recommendation from the investor-as-owner subcommittee on human capital management disclosure*. Securities and Exchange Commission Investor Advisory Committee Retrieved from https://www.sec.gov/spotlight/investor-advisory-committee-2012/iac032819-investor-as-owner-subcommittee-recommendation.pdf

Copeland, B. J. (2000). The modern history of computing. In E. N. Zalta (Ed.), *The Stanford Encyclopedia of Philosophy* (Winter 2000 ed.).

Copeland, B. J. (2011). The Manchester computer: a revised history part 2: the baby computer. *IEEE Annals of the History of Computing, 33*(1), 22–37. doi:10.1109/MAHC.2010.2

Cummings, S. L. (2001). Community economic development as progressive politics: toward a grassroots movement for economic justice. *Stanford Law Review, 54*(3), 399–494.

David, P. A. (1985). Clio and the economics of QWERTY. *American Economic Review, 75*(2), 332–337.

DeTienne, D. R., & Chandler, G. N. (2004). Opportunity identification and its role in the entrepreneurial classroom: a pedagogical approach and empirical test. *Academy of Management Learning & Education, 3*(3), 242–257. doi:10.5465/AMLE.2004.14242103

Dixon, D. P. (2014). *Staying alive: the experience of in extremis leadership*. (Unpublished doctoral dissertation), Case Western Reserve University, Cleveland, OH.

Dixon, D. P., Boland, R., Weeks, M. R., & Gaskin, J. (2014). Leading to live: factors affecting team outcomes in near-death encounters. In M. Warkentin (Ed.), *Trends and Research in the Decision Sciences: Best Papers from the 2014 Annual Conference* (pp. 175–206). Upper Saddle River, NJ: Pearson Education.

Dixon, D. P., Miscuraca, J. A., & Koutroumanis, D. A. (2018). Looking strategically to the future of restaurants: casual dining or fast casual? *Entrepreneurship Education and Pedagogy, 1*(1), 102–117. doi:10.1177/2515127417737288

Dixon, D. P., Weeks, M. R., Boland, R., & Perelli, S. (2017). Making sense when it matters most: an exploratory study of leadership in extremis. *Journal of Leadership & Organizational Studies, 24*(3), 294–317. doi:10.1177/1548051816679356

Endsley, M. R. (1995). Toward a theory of situation awareness in dynamic systems. *Human Factors*, 37(1), 32–64. doi:10.1518/001872095779049543

Farmer, S. M., Yao, X., & Kung-Mcintyre, K. (2011). The behavioral impact of entrepreneur identity aspiration and prior entrepreneurial experience. *Entrepreneurship Theory and Practice, 35*(2), 245–273. doi:10.1111/j.1540-6520.2009.00358.X

Fauconnier, G. (1994). *Mental spaces: aspects of meaning construction in natural language.* Cambridge, UK: Cambridge University Press.

Ferguson, J. W. (2003). Learning from Marriott's exit: company's brand lent credibility to the industry. Assisted living now awaits a new giant. *Assisted Living Today, 10,* 35–36.

Ferguson, J. W. (2005). Anatomy of a turnaround: where strategy and tactics meet. *Seniors Housing & Care Journal, 13*(1), 73–81.

Fiet, J. O. (2002). *The systematic search for entrepreneurial discoveries.* Westport, CT: Quorum Books.

Fisher, M. (2013). *A theory of viral growth of social networking sites.* (Unpublished doctoral dissertation), Case Western Reserve University, Cleveland, OH.

Fisher, M., Abbot, M., & Lyytinen, K. (2013). *The power of customer misbehavior: drive growth and innovation by learning from your customers.* London, UK: Palgrave Macmillan.

General Electric. (2015, September). The digital twin. Could this be the 21st-century approach to productivity enhancements? (GE look ahead). *The Economist.*

Giddens, A. (1986). *The constitution of society: outline of the theory of structuration.* Berkley, CA: University of California Press.

Glaessgen, E., & Stargel, D. (2012). *The digital twin paradigm for future NASA and U.S. Air Force vehicles.* Paper presented at the 53rd AIAA/ASME/ASCE/AHS/ASC Structures, Structural Dynamics and Materials Conference, Honolulu, HI.

Goldsmith, M. (2000). *Learning journeys: top management experts share hard-earned lessons on becoming great mentors and leaders.* Mountain View, CA: Davies-Black.

Gopinath, V., Srija, A., & Neethu Sravanthi, C. (2019). Re-design of smart homes with digital twins. *Journal of Physics: Conference Series, 1228,* doi:10.1088/1742-6596/1228/1/012031

Grayson, K., Johnson, D., & Chen, D-F. R. (2008). Is firm trust essential in a trusted environment? How trust in the business context influences customers. *Journal of Marketing Research*, 45(2), 241–256. doi:10.1509/jmkr.45.2.241

Grieves, M. W. (2002). Conceptual ideal for PLM [PowerPoint presentation]. Product Lifecycle Management Special Meeting, University of Michigan Lurie Engineering Center.

Grieves, M. W. (2005). Product lifecycle management: the new paradigm for enterprises. *International Journal of Product Management*, 2(1/2), 71–84. doi:10.1504/IJPD.2005.006669

Grieves, M. W. (2006). *Product lifecycle management: driving the next generation of lean thinking*. New York, NY: McGraw-Hill.

Grieves, M. W. (2011). *Virtually perfect: driving innovative and lean products through product lifecycle management*. Cocoa Beach, FL: Space Coast Press.

Grieves, M. W. (2019). Virtually intelligent product systems: digital and physical twins. In S. Flumerfelt, K. G. Schwartz, D. Mavris, & S. Briceno (Eds.), *Complex Systems Engineering: Theory and Practice* (pp. 175–200). Reston, VA: American Institute of Aeronautics & Astronautics.

Grieves, M. W., & Vickers, J. (2017). Digital twin: mitigating unpredictable, undesirable emergent behavior in complex systems. In F-J. Kahlen, S. Flumerfelt, & A. Alves (Eds.), *Transdisciplinary Perspectives on Complex Systems: New Findings and Approaches* (pp. 85–113). Cham, Switzerland: Springer International Publishing.

Hajrullina, A. D., & Romadanova, O. A. (2014). Technique of measurement of value of the human capital as intangible asset of corporation. *Life Science Journal*, 11(6s), 518–521.

Hallowell, R. (1996). The relationships of customer satisfaction, customer loyalty, and profitability: an empirical study. *International Journal of Service Industry Management*, 7(4), 27–42.

Hanks, J. (2015). *Operation lock and the war rhino poaching*. Cape Town, South Africa: Penguin Books.

Harris, L. C., & Goode, M. M. H. (2004). The four levels of loyalty and the pivotal role of trust: a study of online service dynamics. *Journal of Retailing*, 80(2), 139–158. doi:10.1016/j.jretai.2004.04.002

Harvard Law School. (2019). John Coates. Retrieved from https://hls.harvard.edu/faculty/directory/10170/Coates/

Ill. H. B. 3394 (101st Gen. Assembly), 805 ILCS 5/8.12 new (Ill. Stat. 2019).

Jackson Jr., J. L. (2001). *Harlemworld: doing race and class in contemporary black America*. Chicago, IL: The University of Chicago Press.

Jacoby, T., & Siegel, F. (1999). Growing the inner city? *New Republic, 221*(8), 22–27.

KPMG LLP. (2017). Audit 2025: the future is now. In *Forbes Insights*. Jersey City, NJ.

Kuhn, T. S. (1962). *The structure of scientific revolutions*. Chicago, IL: University of Chicago Press.

Kvale, S. (1996). *Interviews: an introduction to qualitative research interviewing*. Thousand Oaks, CA: SAGE Publications.

Lamberton, D. M. (1996). *The economics of communication and information*. Cheltenham, UK: Edward Elgars Publishing.

Lave, J., & Wenger, E. (1991). *Situated learning: legitimate peripheral participation*. Cambridge, UK: Cambridge University Press.

Lawrence, K. A., Lenk, P., & Quinn, R. E. (2009). Behavioral complexity in leadership: the psychometric properties of a new instrument to measure behavioral repertoire. *The Leadership Quarterly, 20*(2), 87–102. doi:10.1016/J.LEAQUA.2009.01.014

Leveson, N. G. (1995). *Safeware: system safety and computers*. Boston, MA: Addison-Wesley.

Lobell, J., Sikka, M., & Menon, P. (2015). *Meeting the job challenges of nonprofit leaders: a fieldbook on strategies and action*. Greensboro, NC: CCL Press.

Locke, J. (1998). *An essay concerning humane understanding*. In R. Woolhouse (Ed.), An essay concerning human understanding (Revised ed.). London, UK: Penguin. (Original work published 1690).

Machlup, F. (1983). Semantic quirks in studies of information. In F. Machlup & U. Mansfeld (Eds.), *The study of information: interdisciplinary messages* (pp. 641–671). New York, NY: John Wiley & Sons.

Maher, D. (2018). *On software standards and solutions for a trusted internet of things*. Paper presented at the 51st Hawaii International Conference on System Sciences (HICSS-51), Waikoloa, HI.

Markowska, M., Härtel, C. E. J., Brundin, E., & Roan, A. (2015). A dynamic model of entrepreneurial identification and dis-identification: an emotions perspective. In C. Härtel, E. J., W. J. Zerbe, & N. M. Ashkanasy (Eds.), *New Ways of Studying Emotions in Organizations* (Vol. 11, pp. 215–239): Emerald Publishing Limited.

McMullen, J. S., & Shepherd, D. A. (2006). Entrepreneurial action and the role of uncertainty in the theory of the entrepreneur. *Academy of Management Review, 31*(1), 132–152. doi:10.5465/AMR.2006.19379628

Moses, C. T. (2002). *"Newtown stationary": getting communities back into the economic development game.* (Unpublished qualitative research thesis), Case Western Reserve University, Cleveland, OH.

Moses, C. T. (2003). *Inner city economic empowerment: a tale of two cities.* (Unpublished qualitative research thesis), Case Western Reserve University, Cleveland, OH.

Moses, C. T. (2004a). *Entrepreneurial emergence: key congruence factors and community factors.* (Unpublished quantitative research thesis), Case Western Reserve University, Cleveland, OH.

Moses, C. T. (2004b). *Entrepreneurial emergence: the challenge of growth in urban contexts.* (Unpublished doctoral dissertation), Case Western Reserve University, Cleveland, OH.

Moses, C. T., & Vest, D. (2010). Entrepreneurial emergence: key congruence factors and community processes. *International Journal of Business and Economics Perspectives, 4*(Spring).

Neck, H. M., Neck, C. P., & Murray, E. L. (2017). *Entrepreneurship: the practice and mindset* (1st ed.). Thousand Oaks, CA: SAGE Publications.

Pearce, J. L. (2016). *Organizational behavior: real research for real managers* (4th ed.). Irvine, CA: Melvin & Leigh.

Pendleton-Jullian, A. M., & Brown, J. S. (2018). *Design unbound: designing for emergence in a white water world* (Vol. 1). Cambridge, MA: MIT Press.

Pennington, J., Salin, V., & Dixon, D. P. (2019). *Leadership is the key: a case study of women farmers in Kenya.* Paper presented at the 29th World Conference of the International Food and Agribusiness Management Association (IFAMA), Hangzhou, China.

Piascik, B., Vickers, J., Lowry, D., Scotti, S., Stewart, J., & Calomino, A. (2010). *Technology area 12: materials, structures, mechanical systems, and manufacturing roadmap.* NASA Office of the Chief Technologist.

Poniewozik, J. (2019, May 18). 'Game of Thrones.' Is Going Out Fighting. So Will Its Audience. Retrieved from https://www.nytimes.com/2019/05/18/arts/television/game-of-thrones-season-8.html

Post, J., Groen, M., & Klaseboer, G. (2017). *Physical model based digital twins in manufacturing processes.* Paper presented at the Forming Technology Forum 2017, Enschede, The Netherlands.

Putnam, R. D. (2000). *Bowling alone: the collapse and revival of American community.* New York, NY: Simon & Schuster.

Reichheld, F. F. (2003). The one number you need to grow. *Harvard Business Review, 81*(12), 46–54.

Renzi, D., Maniar, D., McNeill, S., & Del Vecchio, C. (2017). *Developing a digital twin for floating production systems integrity management.* Paper presented at the Offshore Technology Conference. Rio de Janeiro, Brazil.

Rotter, J. B. (1966). Generalized expectancies for internal versus external control of reinforcement. *Psychological Monographs: General and Applied, 80*(1), 1–28. doi:10.1037/H0092976

Salipante, P., & Aram, J. D. (2003). Managers as knowledge generators: the nature of practitioner-scholar research in the nonprofit sector. *Nonprofit Management & Leadership, 14*(2), 129–150. doi:10.1002/nml.26

Salminen, J., & Hytönen, A. (2012, November). *Viral coefficient — unveiling the holy grail of online marketing.* Paper presented at the Conference of Theoretical and Applied Aspects of Cybernetics, Kiev, Ukraine.

Sen, A. K. (1999). *Development as freedom.* New York, NY: Anchor Books.

Shane, S. A. (2004). *Finding fertile ground: identifying extraordinary opportunities for new ventures.* Upper Saddle River, NJ: Pearson Education.

Shapiro, F. R. (2000). Origin of the term software: evidence from the JSTOR electronic journal archive. *IEEE Annals of the History of Computing, 22*(2), 69–71.

Simon, H. A. (1996). *The sciences of the artificial.* Cambridge, MA: MIT Press.

Simon, R., & Barr, C. (2015, January 2). Endangered species: young U.S. entrepreneurs; new data underscore financial challenges and low tolerance for risk among young Americans. *The Wall Street Journal Online.* Retrieved from https://www.wsj.com/articles/endangered-species-young-u-s-entrepreneurs-1420246116

Sirdeshmukh, D., Singh, J., & Sabol, B. (2002). Consumer trust, value, and loyalty in relational exchanges. *Journal of Marketing, 66*(1), 15–37. doi:10.1509/jmkg.66.1.15.18449

Stahl, G. K., & Voigt, A. (2008). Do cultural differences matter in mergers and acquisitions? A tentative model and examination. *Organization Science, 19*(1), 160–176. doi:10.1287/orsc.1070.0270

Stryker, S., & Burke, P. J. (2000). The past, present, and future of an identity theory. *Social Psychology Quarterly, 63*(4), 284–297. doi:10.2307/2695840

The Thirty Percent Coalition. Companies that have appointed a woman to their board since the beginning of 2012. Retrieved from https://www.30percentcoalition.org/simplepagemenu/companies-that-have-appointed-a-woman-to-their-board-since-the-beginning-of-2012

Tuegel, E. J. (2012). *The airframe digital twin: some challenges to realization*. Paper presented at the 53rd AIAA/ASME/ASCE/AHS/ASC Structures, Structural Dynamics and Materials Conference, Honolulu, HI.

Turing, A. M. (1950). Computing machinery and intelligence. *Mind*, 59(236), 433–460.

Useem, M. (2003). Corporate governance is directors making decisions: reforming the outward foundations for inside decision making. *Journal of Management & Governance*, 7(3), 241–253. doi:10.1023/A:1025001307479

Utterback, J. M. (1994). *Mastering the dynamics of information*. Boston, MA: Harvard Business School Press.

Van de Ven, A. H. (2007). *Engaged scholarship: a guide for organizational and social research*. Oxford, UK: Oxford University Press.

Vest, D., & Moses, C. T. (2007). Internationalizing the business faculty via an international spring tour: implications for AACSB accredited historically black college and university business programs. *Global Digital Business Review*, 2(1), 13–18.

Warwick, G. (2014, August 14). Digital twin would track aircraft health through its life. *Aviation Week & Space Technology*. Retrieved from https://aviationweek.com/commercial-aviation/digital-twin-would-track-aircraft-health-through-its-life

Weick, K. E. (1995). *Sensemaking in organizations*. Thousand Oaks, CA: SAGE Publications.

Wolberg, A. (2017). When generals consume intelligence: the problems that arise and how they solve them. *Intelligence & National Security*, 32(4), 460–478. doi:10.1080/02684527.2016.1268359

Zeithaml, V. A., Parasuraman, A. P., & Berry, L. L. (1990). *Delivering quality service: balancing customer perceptions and expectations*. New York, NY: Simon & Schuster.